PENLEE LIFEBOAT

The First 200 Years

Michael Sagar-Fenton

PUBLISHED BY THE PENLEE BRANCH OF THE RNLI

Published by the Penlee Branch of the Royal National Lifeboat Institution 2005.

Penlee Lifeboat Station
The Boathouse
Newlyn Harbour
Newlyn
Penzance
Cornwall
TR18 6HW

www.penleelifeboat.co.uk

ISBN: 978-0-9508611-1-1

Printed in Cornwall by:
Headland Printers, Bread street, Penzance, Cornwall TR18 2EQ

This volume is funded by loans from friends and supporters of Penlee.
It is dedicated to them, and to all those others, past and present,
who have written their names into the station's history.

Introduction and Acknowledgements

This book follows in a proud tradition, being the fourth edition of the history of the Penzance/Newlyn/Penlee lifeboat station.

I was originally asked to update the last edition, the excellent "Penlee Lifeboat" by John Corin and Grahame Farr, published by the branch in 1983. That book concluded with the full impact of the loss of *Solomon Browne* and the subsequent arrival of *Mabel Alice*. However several of the current crew were not even born when those momentous events occurred, and *Mabel Alice* has come and gone, her splendid career so far unrecorded. In order to give a balanced account I therefore decided to rewrite the history in full. This book includes the history of the lifeboat station, followed by a complete service record of *Mabel Alice,* and the previous service record of the station. As the first purpose-built lifeboat was stationed at Penzance in 1803, I have called this edition "Penlee Lifeboat - The First 200 Years", which takes it up to the arrival of the Severn Class *Ivan Ellen* and the inshore Atlantic 75 *Paul Alexander.*

For many readers the name of Penlee will always be associated with disaster and loss. However while the memory of that terrible event will never fade, the work of lifesaving at Penlee has never ceased and continues to go from strength to strength. It is a well-equipped successful modern lifeboat station with a first-class crew, an experienced shore establishment, and no shortage of new volunteers, looking forward to the challenges of the future.

This edition is funded, like its predecessors, by voluntary loans from our friends and supporters. It is not possible to list them all as many wish to remain anonymous, but without them this volume could not have appeared. Their contribution will benefit the branch for years to come and I thank them on behalf of everyone at Penlee for their tremendous generosity.

I would like to thank all those who have helped to bring the project to fruition, all the officers, crew, committee, fund-raisers and helpers, as well as past members and crew, especially those who read the book in manuscript, also to the staff in the archive section at Poole and the welcome hospitality of the Lifeboat College. I would particularly like to thank those who have lent photographs from their own collections along with their memories. A special word for Mr Nicholas Leach of Birmingham whose unsolicited package containing the amazing photographs you see on the front and rear covers arrived just when I was looking for something special. Thanks are also due to Headland Printers, especially Linda Williams for putting the book into a manageable form, to Simon Turney for wading through the manuscript, long lists and all, to correct the proofs, and to Ivan & Heather Corbett of Truran books for their help. I believe the book is as accurate as possible, but I apologise in advance if any errors have been included.

All proceeds of this book, after repayment of the interest-free loans which funded its publication, will be donated to the Penlee Branch of the RNLI.

Michael Sagar-Fenton

FOREWORD

"It is pitch dark, with thick clouds and lashing rain. The wind is still increasing, howling through the empty poles and loose stays, cracking the torn remnants of sail like whips. The ship has been running before the storm all day and most of the night.

A change in the pitch of the seas gives the master his first warning. Soundings are impossible in such conditions, so he releases an anchor, and it catches. But it cannot hold. As the night wears on a new sound comes through the storm, the low roaring of surf beating against a rocky shore. Before dawn the boat takes the ground for the first time, and the bumps become harder and more sudden. Then comes the sound everyone is dreading, the grinding crashing splintering from deep below, sudden jarring movements, jerks and more splintering as the vessel beds into its rocky cradle. All hands are on deck as the ship fills up with frightening speed. There is little comfort there. The ship has itself become a reef, caught fast, and now another obstacle for the breaking seas which run across the deck as if it were a beach.

The masts still stand, the only place above the water's reach. But masts are designed to sway with the movement of the ship not to stand alone, and - undermined below and assaulted above - are soon rocking in their beds with every wave.

The master had fired his forward gun as soon as he realised his peril, but with little hope of assistance. The dawn breaks, and the sailors have their first glimpse of their surroundings, a wall of jagged granite cliffs bursting with spray, interspersed by a few pale beaches. On the nearest beach a small crowd has gathered, waiting - as the crew guess - for the welcome bounty a shipwreck brings. The crew expect no help. The waves are steep and breaking, the wind is screaming, their ship is stuck fast, with other reefs and rocks appearing like teeth from the troughs around them. As the swing of the masts increases, they prepare to die.

And then, from the knot of people on the beach, rising almost vertically with every crest, an open rowing boat full of men begins its short but desperate journey towards them..."

CHAPTER ONE

On the map the Land's End peninsula seems remote, a long limb thrust into the Atlantic, out of the way. But the main era of land transport is only a couple of centuries old. Before that all major journeys were taken by sea. Whether the cargo consisted of passengers, goods, slaves or armies, the sea was the only highway. When the sea is the highway, the Land's End peninsula is suddenly not remote at all but absolutely central. All traffic plying around the west of the British Isles must take account of it. For all those voyaging between the ancient Celtic nations of Ireland and Brittany; approaching from the Bay of Biscay, the west of France, Spain, the Azores, the Balearics; and later all those making their first landfall after crossing the Atlantic, the cliffs and coasts of West Penwith were something to reckon with, and to fear.

Crossing open oceans in sailing boats was a brave but hazardous way to make a living. It was hard even when the weather was favourable, but in poor conditions with minimal navigational aids it was easy to make a fatal mistake. Land's End invited such miscalculations, and punished them heavily. Some ships struck the peninsula because they simply didn't know where they were. Some foundered in the fierce tide-races where the two seas meet. Many others fell foul of the sprinkling of rocks which ensured that the tip of Cornwall had an evil reputation. Now lights and buoys warn of the Longships, the lonely Wolf Rock, the Seven Stones, The Runnelstone, The Bucks, and others, but then they could suddenly appear roaring out of the darkness, just a couple of waves away. It required not only skill, but luck too.

Mounts Bay is a natural haven from the prevailing Atlantic winds, the westerlies and south-westerlies. Once the forbidding cliffs have been safely passed, the bay opens out its arms and a safe anchorage can be found under the lee of the granite plateau, while storms blow themselves out against the Lizard. But the generous arms can also quickly turn into a deadly embrace. We are used to watching weather patterns from satellites in space which show the progress of a spiral depression as it passes through. But sailing ships at anchor in Mounts Bay had no such luxuries, and could never predict

The loss of the *Diana* off Penzance Quay. (Engraving D Blewett collection).

1

when, between one tide and the next, the fierce winds from which they were so successfully sheltering might suddenly swing round and blow equally hard from the opposite direction. Then they really were in trouble. With Land's End out of reach in one direction and The Lizard impossibly far in the other, there was nowhere to go. It was described, with reason, as a maritime trap.

Some entered it deliberately for shelter; some blundered into it in gales or fog; others made the cardinal error of mistaking Land's End for The Lizard and turned northward under the impression they were entering Falmouth Roads. Mostly they succeeded in dodging to and fro or holding anxiously at anchor until the danger was past. But for the unlucky ones the desperate battle was lost and the ships were driven ashore. Some hit the few areas of sand which are not dotted with rocks and stayed more or less in one piece. But the majority found unyielding granite instead, and came to land in many pieces. The pleasant shores of Mounts Bay, where people now laze on summer days, carry a grim history as the graveyard of many fine vessels, and many brave men.

As old as the history of shipwreck is the tradition of heroic assistance from the shore. Most accounts of maritime disaster, however ancient, include awed tributes to those who risked death or injury to deprive the sea of its victims. There is something about the sea which turns all men into brothers, helping each other when they can, banding together against its uncaring moods, and if necessary abandoning all caution to save each other from the common enemy. The legend of Cornish wrecking - deliberate enticement of ships to their doom with false lights etc - still endures, although there is no evidence for a single case. There are on the other hand countless stories of selfless heroism.

A typical example was the wreck of the schooner *Rival* off St Ives on Christmas Eve in 1838. Rescue attempts were made all day in bitter weather by three pilot gigs, two seine boats, another gig which was capsized and driven ashore, a pilchard tow-boat which was also thrown ashore after two of its crew had been washed overboard and almost drowned, and another tow-boat, until, as the light was fading, a pilot gig finally succeeded in taking off the crew of five. None of the rescuers were part of any organisation, but simply determined that the sea should not have its prey.

A wreck might be a godsend to a poor community, but before the well-organised business of plunder could begin, the survivors were the first priority. For many years the law dictated that a vessel was not a total wreck while any of its crew remained alive, an inducement to stand back and let nature take its course. But in a community where so many members were themselves sailors, it was more than flesh and blood could bear to watch the plight of desperate men, often only a few dozen yards away, without doing all they could to help.

So the formation of the Royal National Institution for the Preservation of Life from Shipwreck in 1824 was not an entirely new initiative, but the formal recognition and organisation of a noble tradition. It is impossible to chart the history of the lifeboat service in Mounts Bay without first paying tribute to many other brave men in a line stretching back before history who also answered the call, though their names, their boats, and the details of their services will never be recorded.

CHAPTER TWO

The year of 1803 is an early date in the history of lifeboat institutions. Penzance's need was however felt to be very great. It was a strategic port, though a shadow of what it would become when linked to England by railway. It handled a good deal of tin and other freight, manufactured goods, passengers, and most of the local fishing fleet, as well as those seeking a landfall while on passage. Newlyn was still confined to its old medieval harbour and was tiny by comparison.

Penzance itself had only a single pier, the first 170' of what is now the South Quay, and in bad weather it was difficult to enter and gave only limited protection when inside. There were shipwrecks almost every winter, and after a particularly bad series of losses a letter appeared in the Royal Cornwall Gazette inviting local worthies to add to a substantial grant from Lloyds in order to raise the sum of £150 to equip Penzance with its first purpose-built lifeboat. This was a Henry Greathead "Original", a revolutionary self-righting design, the first boat designed specifically for life-saving. Greathead's boat was 30' long with ten oars, steeply raked at bow and stern, with compartments packed with cork for buoyancy even when swamped. Penzance's boat was stationed with some ceremony on the sandy bank approximately where the railway station now stands.

And that, sadly, is where she stayed.

A Greathead 'Original', in service at Redcar. (RNLI archive).

It is not entirely clear why the locals failed to take to the "Original". She was built at South Shields for work on the east coast. Her design was quite different from Cornish fishing boats, and - particularly in the extreme conditions in which her services would normally be required - the fishermen of Penzance were obviously unwilling to take a chance and put to sea in an unfamiliar boat. It is also likely that the provision of the lifeboat had been considered an end in itself, and the necessity for ongoing practice and training, or even the maintenance of a regular crew, were matters not envisaged by the sponsors. The lifeboat lay unused for nine years, and was eventually auctioned off for twenty guineas. Mounts Bay's first experiment in lifeboat-keeping ended in an ignominious retreat.

Winters continued to bring bad weather, shipping still crowded in and out of Mounts Bay, and rescues carried on as they always had, using pilot gigs and fishing boats and whatever crews were available. It was not until 1824 that another attempt was made to formalise rescue work. The establishment of the RNIPLS was a revolution which laid down some basic principles - the structure of local branches with a central co-ordinating committee, the appointment of officers to instruct and oversee training, maintenance and efficiency, the notion of a semi-permanent group of local volunteers with a coxswain, crew and shore helpers, fund-raising committees, in fact many of the basic guidelines which are still at the core of the RNLI. Local areas were encouraged to form their own branches, and Penzance was amongst the first to sign up. On May 19th 1824 the branch now known as Penlee was officially born.

Another two years were to pass before the branch had a lifeboat of its own, but in 1826 a 24' lifeboat designed by William Plenty, together with carriage, arrived on station. Unfortunately Penzance lifeboat service records do not exist earlier than 1858, and so the first official rescues are not recorded. However there is reason to think that this lifeboat, like its predecessor, was not received with great enthusiasm by those appointed to man it. Newspaper accounts of shipwreck in Mounts Bay continue to refer to rescues by familiar local vessels for at least another generation. The 'Plenty' lifeboat was said to have been shipwrecked itself, probably in 1827, so presumably it had at least a taste of active service.

The enthusiasm for a lifeboat service was kept alive mainly by the local Lloyds agent Richard Pearce who was also Honorary Secretary of the branch - not the last character to hold those two posts. Pearce had himself played a central part in the rescue of six men from the brig *Albion* which had been wrecked off Newlyn Green in 1828, and was awarded the institution's silver medal in 1851 for his record of services. His persistence was eventually rewarded in 1853 when funds for a new lifeboat - again to the tune of £150 - were raised locally, and a new boat was built for Penzance. It was also built in Penzance, by shipwrights Semmens and Thomas, a 'Peake' type, 30' long, 8' beam, with ten oars and a crew of 12. It has the distinction of performing the first recorded service, on 7th October 1858, to stand by the schooner *Hopewell* off Penzance during a gale.

The middle years of the century had seen a huge expansion Penzance's fortunes and pretensions. The town itself tripled in population between 1801 and 1871, and the arrival of the railways in 1859 opened the door to trade in one direction and tourism in the other. After many false starts, the Albert Pier was finished in 1848, and the South Quay was extended to its current length in 1855. Many other developments were taking place, turning Penzance into a fashionable and successful town, enjoying the fruits of shipping and industry, a market town and a resort. In the further corner of the bay Newlyn was still regarded as a poor relation, a working class fishing port, and its requests for permission to extend its own harbour were continually quashed by petitions to parliament from the burghers of Penzance. Amongst the less notable new buildings around Penzance harbour was a modest lifeboat house, erected at a cost of £88 near the old berth by the railway station.

In the prosperous years of the Victorian age philanthropy of all kinds gained a new status, and the selfless attitude of the RNLI (the shorter title adopted by the RNIPLS in 1854) appealed to the new mood of sentimental celebration of charitable deeds and noble acts. While the 'Peake' type had slipped into service after a long struggle to raise funds, the arrival of Penzance's next lifeboat was quite a different kettle of fish.

Richard Lewis launches to the barque *North Britain* 1868. (RNLI archive).

CHAPTER 3

"The Mayor and Corporation now headed the procession which wended its way by the chapel wall and Sandybank to the Green. The whole Green from the Station to the Baths was crowded with people, not one of whom budged during a brief but pitiless shower... The Lady Mayoress approached the bows of the lifeboat, the bottle of foaming champagne was dashed against her bows with the emphatic words "God speed the Alexandra ", and the boat was launched."

Those now tasked with organising the naming ceremony of a new lifeboat would be grateful they were not available in 1863. The new lifeboat was another 'Peake' style, though smaller and finer than her predecessor. Her naming was part of the celebrations commemorating the marriage of the Prince of Wales to Princess Alexandra of Denmark (who also lent her name to the road leading from Alverton to the seafront).

The order of the procession is worth recording in full:

> St Buryan Artillery Band
> Coastguards, Royal Naval Reserve, and Pensioners
> The Lifeboat "Alexandra" and crew
> St Buryan Artillery
> Penzance Brass Band
> The 1st Duke of Cornwall's Rifles
> Oddfellows with their Regalia
> Morvah Band
> Members of the Weslyan Provident Society
> Foresters in Full Costume
> Penzance Drum & Fife Band
> The Danish Standard
> The British Standard and Ensign
> The Town Arms, Sergeants at Mace, Town Clerk
> and Clerk of the Peace
> Mayor and Justices
> Corporation, Clergy, Magistrates, Officers of HM Customs
> Towednack Band
> Trinity Men (a body of 45 craftsmen involved in the building of the
> new lighthouse on the Wolf Rock)
> New Mill Band
> Police

The *Alexandra* had in fact been in service some three years before this formal occasion, and was the first Penzance lifeboat to be honoured with a name. Her only recorded service was a splendid one, to the brig *Willie Ridley* which was dragging her anchors ashore on Eastern Green in a fierce SE storm and heavy seas. The *Alexandra* was commanded by the local Coastguard Inspector, Captain Fellowes in the absence of the regular coxswain. She made a number of efforts to launch from the beach, but was driven back onto the sands and then the rocks, breaking several oars in the process.

Eventually she was re-berthed on her carriage and towed to Newlyn. After some "hard rowing" they succeeded in reaching the brig, and took off the captain and seven crew. Captain Fellowes was awarded the Institution's Silver Medal. The *Willie Ridley* was later recovered and continued on her voyage.

A few days later the *Alexandra* was herself on her way. She had been too light for the rigours required of her, and was replaced by a 32' self-righting lifeboat with a crew of 13 rather than 8, and at 2 tons, nearly twice the *Alexandra's* weight. Most of her £210 cost was borne by Mr J Chamberlain of Birmingham, but, with his agreement, she was named after the Secretary of the RNLI, Richard Lewis. With the *Richard Lewis* the story of Penzance lifeboats as a truly effective force in saving lives in Mounts Bay really begins.

She did not undertake the task alone. The RNLI was expanding fast, its new popularity attracting funds from benevolent societies and landed gentry all around the coasts of Britain. By 1867 the 'great maritime trap' between The Lizard and Lands End was defended by no less than five lifeboats: Sennen Cove, Penzance, Porthleven, Mullion and The Lizard. The last three were instigated and supported by T J Agar-Robartes Esq of Lanhydrock. Helston provided further assistance in the form of Henry Trengrouse, who had been so shocked by the loss of life at the wreck of the Frigate *Anson* on Loe Bar in 1807 that he had spent his life perfecting and promoting a rocket-propelled rescue apparatus which saved many lives close to shore.

The famous lifeboat races of 1867, including crews from Penzance, St Ives, Sennen, Porthleven, Hayle and the new station at Mullion (RNLI archive).

Lifeboats had no early-warning system with which to detect a growing crisis. The first signs of trouble might be cannon-fire or rockets, but would usually be a visual report, and since trouble often meant heavy weather and poor visibility, there were few opportunities to launch in time to prevent disaster. Boats which foundered offshore did so alone and unrecorded, their tragedy known only when they failed to come to land or their wreckage was discovered. The casualties which called for a lifeboat's services in the 19th century were therefore typically vessels which had run before a storm and driven or dragged anchor until they stranded on whichever part of the shore fate decreed. It might be soft sand or an offshore reef, and the speed of their destruction varied accordingly.

The distances from shore were never very great, just a few yards in some cases, but disproportionately dangerous. Wrecks were nearly always stuck amongst the breakers, where the steep and unpredictable waves stood boats virtually up on end, and could swamp them in a moment. Launching a two-ton lifeboat together with its 13 crew, ready at the oar, from a heavy trailer in soft sand required a huge amount of effort, strength and skill from the large launching party, in real danger of being swept away themselves. Their efforts were often in vain as a breaker threw the lifeboat sideways and, before she could recover, the next wave swamped her and often broke the oars of the crew who were struggling to save her from capsize. There was nothing to prevent the crew themselves from being swept away as the vessel broached. Accounts tell of many such attempts in succession, despite cold and exhaustion, until the boat was either launched or hauled back onto its carriage and taken laboriously to a more promising launching site.

Detail from the launch of *Richard Lewis* to the barque *North Britain*. (RNLI archive).

Ashore the beach would be filled with the crowd of helpers, would-be rescuers, officials and observers, wives and families watching desperately, children, horses and dogs, often lit by lanterns in the dark, always in the teeth of the wind accompanied with driving rain and spray, all eyes on the small open rowing-boat on which all hopes rested

Once the lifeboat was under way she was fully exercised in keeping her bows up to the weather, pulling when able in the cresting seas. But the greatest hazards awaited her when 'on scene'. The wreck would be fast on either shallow ground or a reef, and the lifeboat had to negotiate not only the surrounding rocks but also the ropes, rigging, timbers and possibly cargo from the wreck which would be tossing in the water, creating an additional threat and impeding clear progress. As she closed with the casualty, the nearside oars would have to be shipped, losing at once half of her power and manoeuvrability at the crucial moment. All co-ordination of the oarsmen would have to be instant and precise, on the orders of the coxswain as shouted above the rain, wind and crashing surf, sometimes in near pitch darkness. Add to this the long exposure of the crew, drenched to the skin, often in the middle of winter, and it is easy to see why some of these services still rate amongst the classics of the lifeboat service, and indeed in the general record of man's humanity to man.

CHAPTER 4

Some highlights of the *Richard Lewis* years:

24th NOVEMBER 1865

Richard Lewis was taken on her carriage to Marazion to the aid of the brigantine *Tobaco* of Hamburg, en route to Hamburg with timber. She had driven ashore in heavy SSW gale and tremendous seas which were washing over her, forcing the crew into the rigging. A rocket line was fired but the crew could not reach it, and so the lifeboat was launched. Despite a near capsize she reached the wreck and successfully took off the crew of five.

11th JANUARY 1866

After the wreck of steamship *Bessie* on Lelant Sands in a NE gale, *Richard Lewis* was hauled all the way to Hayle by eight horses in order to assist the St Ives lifeboat *Moses* which had telegrammed for help. Both boats managed to reach the wreck through huge seas and strong tides, the *Moses* recovering three survivors and *Richard Lewis* the remaining six. Coxswain Thomas Carbis was awarded a Silver Medal for his part in the rescue. *

5th JANUARY 1867

Richard Lewis was launched from Long Rock beach in an ESE gale to assist the schooner *Salome* of Brixham which was drifting helplessly ashore. The lifeboat took off the crew of five men and a boy, and soon afterwards the *Salome* struck and was quickly dashed to pieces.

Later the same evening the wind had intensified from the SSE, and blue flashlights were seen from the shore. *Richard Lewis* launched once more, in darkness and heavy rain, first to the schooner *Selina Ann* from which she saved the crew of five despite being nearly overturned while alongside; and then to the schooner *Heiress*, saving the crew of six. Both vessels were wrecked shortly afterwards.

Second Coxswain Samuel Higgs was awarded the Silver Medal and Bowman NB Downing the Thanks on Vellum.

7th JANUARY 1867

Two days later, after reports of a vessel ashore near St Michaels Mount, *Richard Lewis* launched into the darkness at 7pm into a SE gale and "one of the most tremendous seas ever remembered there". She reached the *John Gray* of Glasgow after a heroic pull, and rescued thirteen of the crew with great difficulty. The captain and five of the crew

* It was not the last meeting between "Richard Lewis" and the "Moses". In 1867 a regatta was held in Mounts Bay as part of the celebrations for the newly opened Public Buildings, now better known as St Johns Hall. Six Cornish lifeboats competed in a race, and as the Penzance and St Ives lifeboats rounded the Gear Pole together some of the age-old rivalry between the two towns came to the fore, and a 'fracas' was observed from the shore. While the two crews were thus engaged, the Sennen lifeboat passed them both and went on to win

Artist's impression of *Richard Lewis* returning from the wreck of the *John Grey* on 7th January 1867. (RNLI archive).

insisted on remaining aboard until daylight. The next morning the lifeboat returned to the wreck, but although she managed to get alongside, the captain would not allow his crew to abandon. When a rocket line was successfully fired over her, he threatened to shoot any man who attempted to reach it. As the tide flooded they paid the price for his obstinacy as the ship was quickly broken up and all six were drowned.

6th DECEMBER 1868

At about 2pm "a horseman galloped into Penzance with news of a large vessel in a perilous position in the bay." It was the barque *North Britain* of Southampton, and despite the efforts of a pilot gig and the St Michael's Mount barge to reach her, she went ashore off Marazion in a severe SSW storm. The captain did not see *Richard Lewis* making ready to launch and put his boats out. One was immediately smashed, but the captain managed to launch his jolly-boat with nine crew, leaving eight aboard. The jolly-boat capsized long before reaching shore, and the nine were thrown into the sea. Only three of the survivors came ashore alive, pulled from the waves by local wrestling champion William Jeffery at the head of a human chain, although one died on the beach shortly after. It took *Richard Lewis* an hour to pull to the wreck, and just as she did so she was herself capsized by a "great sea", throwing all her crew into the water and trapping Coxswain Thomas Carbis under the boat. The crew somehow managed to right the lifeboat again and Carbis was brought aboard, apparently dead. Stroke oarsman Edward Hodge was washed away, but was saved by his cork lifebelt and recovered from the surf by G Desreaux who swam his horse out to rescue him. Second Coxswain Higgins brought the lifeboat safely ashore, assisted by Coastguard Inspector Captain R B Cay who was also amongst the crew.

There were still eight to save, and so fresh volunteers were called for. Samuel Higgins, although exhausted, immediately volunteered as did G Desreaux, French Vice-consul Samuel Higgs and others, and a crew was soon assembled with Coastguard Officer W Blackmore as cox. Again she launched into the surf. Several times she was thrown almost vertical by the waves and the watchers thought she must go over again, but yard by yard she managed to reach the wreck and took off the eight survivors. Ten minutes later the *North Britain's* masts went over, and in half an hour she was "in fragments". Thomas Carbis later recovered, and the only injuries were to crewman Anthony Pascoe who broke three ribs.

For this, one of the most noble rescues in the station's history, five Silver Medals were awarded, to Coxswain Carbis, Second Cox Higgins, Captain Cay, Officer Blackmore and Samuel Higgs. Thanks on Vellum were awarded to Messrs Desreaux, Hon Sec N Downing and the wrestler William Jeffery.

The awards were presented at St Johns Hall, pleasingly by Richard Lewis in person.

So the record of the *Richard Lewis* continued. In January 1873 she saved eight people as well as a dog and a pig from the wreck of the brig *Otto*, leading to awards from the government of Norway. In February 1873 she saved the crew of four from the wreck of the *Marie Emilie*, breaking seven oars and being hurled twice onto the deck of the casualty. Silver medals were awarded to N Downing, Captain Howarth and William Blackmore for their part in these two rescues.

The service of May 1879 led to a Gold Medal from the French government. It was to the brig *Ponthieu* of Vannes, ashore off Perranuthnoe with a crew of six. Despite a rocket line being successfully launched and the casualty being approached by both *Richard Lewis* and a local fishing boat, the crew - under the watchful eye of the captain - refused to leave. Eventually, as conditions worsened, the lifeboat managed to persuade all except the captain to come off. They stood by for him for some time but were in considerable danger amongst rocks and, after breaking three oars, made for shore to land the casualties. One of the Marazion coastguards named Gould made a desperate attempt to change the captain's mind by volunteering to take a letter from the French Vice-consul urging him to leave. The only way to do this was by way of the line which had been attached by rocket, and the unfortunate Gould duly hauled himself out to the wreck hand over hand through the most atrocious conditions, surely one of the bravest postmen ever. Having delivered the letter, he was washed off the line on the way back and almost lost, but was rescued from shore in an exhausted state and revived with brandy. However the doughty Breton Captain Kergulant was not to be persuaded even by such heroic means, and it was not until the masts collapsed with him in the rigging that he accepted the inevitable and grasped the rocket line, to be hauled ashore by a human chain. Mr Gould was awarded the Gold Medal.

The days of *Richard Lewis* were drawing to a close. They set a standard for the RNLI which still inspires wonder today.

In 1884 Mr Henry Martin Harvey, JP, of Launceston donated the generous sum of £1000 for the provision of a new lifeboat for Penzance and a brand new boathouse to put her in. *Richard Lewis* was finally retired, to be replaced by the 34' *Dora*.

CHAPTER 5

The location of the boathouse was not then as significant as it later became. The Lifeboat was seldom launched close to her station, but was usually hauled to wherever the wreck happened to be. In 1869 she was even hauled eight miles through floods and broken roads all the way to Praa Sands to the rescue of the barque *Choice*. The age of the five-minute launch would then have been unimaginable. First the crew and shore helpers had to be gathered together. Then the horses had to be rounded up which in the summer could take some time since they were in the fields and had first to be caught. The lifeboat then made its stately procession to the nearest viable launch site, followed by a large crowd.

After 1867 *Richard Lewis* dwelt in a timber boathouse opposite the end of Alexandra Road. Mr Harvey's donation made possible the building of a more substantial and imposing house for the *Dora*. It was made of Lamorna granite and situated beside the Abbey slipway in the innermost part of Penzance harbour. After an initial hiccough - it had to be shifted several feet to the south to avoid taking the light from the small cottages which once neighboured it - a handsome building emerged at a cost of £575. Above the main doors was a granite bell turret bearing two pottery reliefs of the RNLI crest. It was opened in 1885 by the donor.

The Jennings Street Boathouse, built in 1884. (RNLI archive).

Into it went the new 3-ton lifeboat *Dora* to continue the good work of her predecessor. The bay sometimes resounded now to the sound of steam-boats, but sail was still the principal means of propulsion, and the same vulnerability to onshore gales ensured that there was important work to do. The *Dora's* first service had already taken place before the grand opening, to the barque *Petrellen*, taking off most of the crew as a precaution, returning them later to the vessel, and, as the wind increased and her cables parted, taking off her whole complement of ten shortly before the barque was wrecked at Eastern Green.

In the small hours of 8th December 1886 she saved nine lives from two different local vessels the *Alliance* and the *Golden Light*, and she went on to save a further thirty lives in her seven-year record.

However she will always be remembered best for her service of 17th May 1888. It was to the brigantine *Jeune Hortense* of Nantes, which followed many other hapless vessels in dragging her anchors until she grounded on the sands to the west of Marazion. Under coxswain Henry Trewhella, the *Dora* pulled through heavy surf to the wreck and, despite losing all the oars on one side, took off the crew of three men and a boy to safety. The rescue itself was bravely done, but the reason for its fame has less to do with the exceptional features of the service than the presence amongst the crowd of the master of Victorian photography, John Gibson. His panorama of the scene, clearly showing the wreck, the lifeboat, the crowd on the beach, and the high seas, against the unmistakable profile of St Michaels Mount under a lowering sky, has become one of the most famous photographs in the RNLI's records.

May 1888 - the *Dora* returns from the *Jeune Hortense.* (Gibson).

The *Dora* was said by her crew to be "heavy to pull, but a grand sea boat" She was replaced in 1896 by an even heavier boat, a gift of the Misses Smitheram of Albury, the *Elizabeth & Blanche*, which was two feet longer at 36'. A year later Henry Trewhella retired and was awarded a silver medal in recognition of his 'long and gallant services'.

It was becoming the custom to put the lifeboat afloat as a precaution in bad weather, to avoid the heavy work of hauling her across the harbour mud, sometimes almost as far as the harbour mouth, when time was of the essence. This tactic saved a great deal of trouble and also allowed the lifeboat to render service in time to save the vessel, rather than waiting until a wreck was inevitable.

Launching the lifeboat could be relatively expensive. A typical expense account, of Boxing Day 1912, (Launching the *Janet Hoyle* - see below) includes:

13 men @ 15/-
26 helpers @ 3/-
Signalman 3/-
Telephone messenger 3/-
6 horses with drivers £2.4.0
Boss launcher 6/-
7 wet men, 1/- extra

Elizabeth & Blanche was 'upgraded' again as the century turned, to be replaced by *Elizabeth & Blanche II* from the same donors, another two feet longer at 38', and weighing a full five tons. Coxswain Trewhella had retired with the award of the Silver Medal for his long service, to be replaced by Phillip Nicholls.

Elizabeth & Blanche II in service. (Peter & Liz Harris collection).

However George Chirgwin was coxswain on the morning of 14th March 1905. Reports had come in of a large barque, the *Khyber*, which was embayed and desperately riding her anchors off Tol-Pedn Penwith in a furious westerly gale. Not even the strength and determination of the lifeboat's crew could possibly have sailed or rowed *Elizabeth & Blanche II* so far against the wind and sea. However it was more than they could bear to stand by doing nothing except hoping for a change in the wind, and they engaged the services of the steamer *Lady Of The Isles*. Her skipper, Captain Anderson, agreed to tow the lifeboat to the scene. The steamer herself had a hard time of it as she came out of the bay into the teeth of the gale, and the crew of the *Elizabeth & Blanche II* had to undergo a degree of exposure which few modern fishermen, no matter how tough, would survive. Without even the recreation of rowing they had to sit tight and hold on, up to their waists in cold March water, as virtually every wave rolled over them for hour after hour. Eventually they struggled around Gwennap Head, ready to slip the tow and veer down to the casualty. But she was no longer there. The anchors had parted before help could arrive, and the *Khyber* was pounded to matchwood in minutes, with the loss of twenty-two of her crew. Their memorial stands in St Levan churchyard; and one of the most heroic episodes in the station's history does not even appear in the service records.

Steam was rapidly taking over from sail, ships able if necessary to go head to sea to escape the maritime trap, and the number of launches decreased accordingly. However new challenges arose, and on 27th September 1907 *Elizabeth & Blanche II* launched in an ESE gale to carry a doctor to the steamer SS *Ellesmere* near the Runnelstone, and waited until he had done his work before carrying him home again, the station's first recorded 'medico'.

In the same year the perennial problem of shifting five tons of boat plus another ton of crew over the harbour mud before launching led to a controversy. The barge *Baltic*, which was carrying cement for the building of the new north pier at Newlyn went ashore on St Clement's Island off Mousehole in a November fog. The sound of the crew's cries of distress carried through the fog to Mousehole, where they were heard by boatman Stanley Drew. It appears that the lifeboat was subsequently sent for but did not arrive, for reasons not recorded. Since the baulks were down across Mousehole harbour mouth, the harbour crane was commandeered to lift the gig *Lady White* over the harbour wall, where she launched, and soon took off the barge's crew. Fishermen from different ports are never reluctant to tease each other, and the occasion was soon celebrated in verse:

> "Where was the lifeboat when the *Baltic* went ashore?
> They took the *Lady White* and launched her across the por."

Selling the catch in Mousehole harbour (Frank Blewett in the centre).
(D Blewett collection).

A full account ensued:

> "The first to volunteer was Mr Stanley Drew,
> Then came down old Woodall, with his leggings painted blue..."

And so on. The rescue was not particularly hazardous, but a local resident had medals struck for the whole of the gig's crew. Mr Stanley Drew's son Johnny played a significant part in the future history of the lifeboat, and the *Baltic's* mate, Irishman Adam Torrie, came ashore and married the harbour-master's daughter, Janey Blewett, founding another dynasty with crucial lifeboat connections.

Whatever the true circumstances, the event hastened a change which had been long resisted, the stationing of a lifeboat in Newlyn.

CHAPTER 6

Penzance and Newlyn, though close neighbours, had never been friends. Penzance had strenuously opposed any extension of Newlyn's medieval harbour, and it was not until the local fishing boat *Jane* was sunk with all hands off Penzance promenade in 1885 in full view of family and friends that permission was finally granted to create an all-weather harbour of refuge there. Soon after its completion the two communities came to blows during the bitter Newlyn Riots, when Penzance sided with the East-Coast fishermen who had outraged Newlyn by fishing on the Sabbath.

However the forces of common sense and geography eventually overcame Penzance's social disdain. Newlyn was sheltered in almost all weathers with a harbour which never fully dried out. It was, and had always been, the obvious place for a lifeboat. With little of the customary ceremony therefore, *Elizabeth & Blanche II* officially moved stations in 1908 . Newlyn had no boathouse to offer, nor any convenient location to build one, and so the lifeboat lay under a canvas cover on the foreshore beneath the Fisherman's Arms, close to where the trawler repair slipway now lies.

This was regarded as a trial placement only, and the RNLI sent the 34' fifteen-year-old lifeboat *Cape Of Good Hope* to be housed in the Wharf Road boathouse as a reserve. She recorded only one service, to one of the despised East-Coasters, the drifter *Renown* of Yarmouth, which failed to make Penzance harbour mouth in rough weather. After a splendid effort in shallow water the lifeboat managed to take her a rope and brought the other end to the pier head, where hundreds of volunteers hauled the drifter to safety.

Penzance lifeboat *Cape of Good Hope* goes to the aid of the Yarmouth drifter *Renown*, Feb 1909. (Tony Pawlyn Collection).

In 1912, after being damaged in service, she was replaced by another vintage lifeboat the *Janet Hoyle.* Her finest hour - though recorded in the dispassionate statistics of the RNLI as "No service" - was on Boxing Day, 1912. After hearing reports of a steamer driving across the bay, the Penzance lifeboat was launched in SE storm. Winds up to 90 mph were blowing in shop fronts on the seafront, boats were overturning in the harbour and seas were washing right over the pier-head. The open boat under coxswain William Nicholls went out into the storm under sail, swamped by the first wave and almost every wave thereafter, and kept afloat only by the lifeboat's airtight compartments. After a long search to the west and then across towards Porthleven, she was finally recalled. By then their goal, the steamer *Tripolitania*, had been thrown up above high water-mark on Loe Bar, occasioning another of Gibson's famous photographs.

A stand-by service in March 1913 to oversee a number of trawlers running for Penzance in a SSW gale was her last recorded service. The station was officially closed in 1917, and the *Janet Hoyle* was sold at auction, for £13.

Wharf Road boathouse passed to the ownership of Penzance Borough Council, and thence to Penwith District Council, who leased it back to the RNLI. It served as a depot and then commenced a new career as a souvenir shop, as which it did sterling service right up until 1999. At that point the RNLI decided that the cost of repairs did not justify the continuation of the lease, and the historic building was handed back to the Council, in whose hands it remains. A new lease was taken on a former chandlers' shop on the other side of the Ross Bridge, to continue the precious work of fund-raising. But the active service of the Penzance Lifeboat Station had ceased in 1913, after 110 years of endeavour, development and heroic action.

Elizabeth & Blanche II stationed in Newlyn. (RNLI archive).

With the move to Newlyn, lifeboat services continued to gain in variety, and started to resemble the patterns more familiar today. No longer was the call to the boat the last resort when the wreck was already hard ashore, but often a precautionary measure. The lifeboat was called out whenever a boat was seen anchored in a dangerous position, or even when appearing to come heedlessly into the bay. She was launched whenever a gale threatened the fishing fleet, performed escort duties and assisted boats entering the harbour. In 1911, for example, she took provisions to the exhausted crew of the schooner *Lizzie Ellen* which was nearly swamped, and the lifeboat's crew then set to her pumps for four hours, raising her eighteen inches and allowing her to be towed to Falmouth by a steamer.

The position in Newlyn gave her a considerable advantage. It was a far shorter launch over harder ground, and she could usually make good progress to seaward before turning into the body of the bay, rather than having to fight for her life the instant she headed the pier as had so often been the case in Penzance. Radio was coming, giving warning for the first time of casualties beyond the visual limits of watchers on the coast. In 1912 when the steamer *South America* was dangerously close to shore by Merthen Point, the lifeboat was alerted by the novelty of the telephone, though too late to stop her from grounding in St Loy cove.

The *Saluto* hard ashore off Perranuthnoe. (RNLI archive).

But before things changed completely, there was one throwback to the golden age. On 13th December 1911 the SW gale brought up such high seas that the glass in the lighthouse on Newlyn Pier was smashed. In poor visibility the Norwegian barque *Saluto* had made the classic error of mistaking Land's End for Lizard Point and was running into the bay. By the time she discovered her error it was too late to escape. She was driven rapidly eastward towards the rocks. Her plight had been observed, and soon *Elizabeth & Blanche II*, under coxswain T E Vingoe was launched and giving chase across the bay. She caught up with the *Saluto* just in time, perilously close to shore off Perranuthnoe. The barque was rolling so heavily she was sometimes dipping her yard-arms into the sea, and the lifeboat had to drop her sails and lower the masts before she dared make an approach under oars alone. Despite losing four oars, the lifeboat somehow managed to avoid serious damage from the casualty and took off the crew of thirteen with great skill. The rescued crew then joined the regular crew in double-banking the oars to get the lifeboat to seaward away from the hazard of the nearby lee shore. When she had escaped the immediate danger sail was set, and the crowded boat returned through the mighty seas to Newlyn. Tying up at the quay she was greeted by photographers and the Salvation Army Band, playing "Oh God Our Help In Ages Past". Inexplicably no official recognition was made of the rescue, but Coxswain Vingoe was awarded a silver cup by the grateful Norwegian government.

It was the end of an era. No longer would sailing boats come into the bay to be caught like butterflies in a net. Rescues of the future would be of a different nature, if no less demanding.

And what of the crew? The photographs show little: a group of men wrapped in canvas clothes and oilskins encircled by cork belts, never seen bare-headed except in chapel or church, their faces often obscured by a bushy moustache. They gaze out of the photographs with a tough and challenging stare, as well they might. They lived lives of great hardship and frequent poverty, low in the social order, fiercely religious. Hard men. And yet in all accounts of lifeboat work some things never change - the teamwork, the pride, the dedication, the sense of adventure, and above all the wry humour which enabled them to deal with triumph, disaster or fiasco alike. Behind the constant ribbing were men willing to take any chance in order to snatch the helpless from their fate, hard cases ready to care for the injured or frightened as tenderly as a mother with a child, men of few words but ready wit, men of huge experience who often knew more than those who sought to guide them. Lifeboatmen. Not so very different from today.

The 'trial' at Newlyn had obviously been a great success. The next advance was to increase the speed of response even further. Horses had long since ceased to haul the boat to the water, and now men too were to be relieved of this heavy burden. It was clear that lifeboats of the future would also be motor-driven, which would lead to another major increase in weight. As early as 1910 it had been decided to choose a site and proceed to raise the enormous sum of £2850 in order to place a boathouse and a purpose-built slipway on it. The site chosen was east-facing, sheltered in most weathers, and provided a launch into clear water. It was nearer to Mousehole than Newlyn, which gave the lifeboat a great advantage when she had to beat out of the bay against the sea, being (as John Corin notes) "already three tacks to the good". It also changed the makeup of the crew, encouraging the Mousehole men to cease their teasing and take their turn. The first age of the Newlyn lifeboat was already over. The name of the point was adopted as the new name of the station, which it still bears. The Penlee Lifeboat was born.

CHAPTER 7

Penlee lifeboat station. (Andrew Besley).

The idea of launching from a slipway straight into the water was one of the RNLI's greatest inspirations. It overcame the back-breaking work of man-hauling in waist-deep water, and the necessity for a huge launching crew, ensuring that a boat could be on its way in a few minutes rather than a hour or so. But it was also the incidental spectacular value which served the institution so well. The image of the boat speeding down a ramp to enter the water with a mighty and satisfying splash was a potent symbol of the urgency and adventure of every launch, which affected all who saw it, even those who never went near the sea.

However the first practice launch at Penlee was not quite the dignified demonstration it was intended to be. As a tribute to Newlyn's record of achievement the new Mousehole crew stood by and let the Newlyn boys have the honour of the first ride. Penlee is reputed to be the steepest slipway in the country, and on subsequent launches the boat was lowered towards the sea before letting go. However on this occasion the pin was knocked out with the boat still in the boathouse, and the tide at low water. The five tons of *Elizabeth & Blanche II* along with its ton of human complement, including the current and previous Honorary Secretaries, slid down at ever-increasing speed, hit the sea in an explosion of water, and completely disappeared. The watchers gaped in alarm at a hat floating on the surface, the only sign of her passing. The she suddenly rose from the waves a good thirty yards out "like a blowing whale", with everyone still in their places, if drenched to the skin. The Mousehole men, hiding their smiles, took note.

An early launch at Penlee –
Elizabeth & Blanche II goes down with
sails already set. (RNLI archive).

Soon she was going down the slipway in earnest, her first launch in October 1914 to the ss *Liguria* which had lost her propeller. But for four years war service depleted the crews, and no further civilian rescues took place until after it was over. The next significant call was not until November 1918, to the Admiralty tug *Epic* which had stranded in the old ships' graveyard off Long Rock. At first conditions were so appalling that an approach was impossible and a rocket line was attached, but when that too proved impossible to use, the lifeboat went back and managed to take off all seventeen of the crew.

Services were becoming longer, as reports came in from the coastguard radio network of incidents further out at sea. In July 1922 *Elizabeth & Blanche II* launched to assist the ss *Concordia* which was disabled near the Wolf Rock. Several vessels stood by but most hopes were pinned on the St Mary's lifeboat, the first one in the area to be engine-powered. However she broke down after three hours and was obliged to run for Falmouth the old-fashioned way, under sail. The Penlee lifeboat stood by until the wind turned further to the west and the *Concordia's* skipper could risk raising his anchors before accepting a tow from a steamer. The lifeboat returned to Mousehole, her temporary berth during alterations to the boathouse and slipway, after more than seven hours at sea.

It was her last shout. The purpose of the alterations was to house the new engine-powered Watson-type lifeboat, *The Brothers*, and the last of the rowing and sailing lifeboats went into retirement. *Elizabeth & Blanche II* had been one of the great servants of the station, 22 years working in the most demanding conditions, spanning an era between the last of the Victorian age and the technological era of the 1920s. In future new challenges faced the boats and a new range of skills would be required from the crew as well as strong arms and brave hearts.

The new boat was a monster. At 45' she was seven feet longer, and at 12'6, three feet wider than her predecessor. Her weight was a solid 16t 15cwt, which would have taken some hauling over the harbour mud. Her cost was also of a new dimension, £13,214 as opposed to the £753 paid for the *Elizabeth & Blanche II*. The sum was donated by three Misses Eddy of Torquay in memory of their two nephews who had drowned in a boating accident at Cambridge. Miss Amy Eddy named and launched the boat from Penlee, and the remainder of the service of dedication took place off the promenade.

The RNLI had been experimenting with powered lifeboats since 1904. It was a demanding brief, requiring an engine which would continue to perform in a boat swamped with water and even survive a capsize. Steam lifeboats, which required a live fire to be kept alight, were not a success. *The Brothers* power pack was a relatively well-developed 90 bhp 6-cylinder petrol engine. Confidence in engines was not absolute, and full set of sails and oars was still kept on board just in case. Indeed service reports right up until World War II had a space reserved for the choice of propulsion, whether oars, sail, or 'motive power'.

Recovering *The Brothers* at Penlee. (D Blewett collection).

Naturally she was greeted with deep suspicion at Penlee. As the saying goes "It is sea-going human nature patiently to suffer accustomed evils, but to be very intolerant of new difficulties." Looking at her economical design and graceful lines now it is hard to imagine what a revolution she represented.

Handsome is as handsome does, and her first service was a splendid one. In January 1923 the large steamship *Dubravka* of Dubrovnik had lost a propeller near the Runnelstone in a heavy westerly gale and was dragging her anchors towards the reef itself. She pulled up just 20 yards from the rocks, and *The Brothers* had to go in so close to them that seas washed right over her. In these conditions she took off 27 of the crew and packed them into the lifeboat. *Dubravka's* anchor did in the end hold, and she was towed away next morning to live another day.

Later the same year *The Brothers* brought home the largest group of casualties in the station's history. The Runnelstone was once again the cause of the incident. The large steamship *City Of Westminster* was en route to Belfast from Rotterdam with a cargo of maize and 73 passengers and crew aboard. She struck the rock in heavy weather and stuck fast in a heavy ground swell. The Sennen lifeboat *The Newbons* arrived first and took off three women and ten of the crew. There seemed little prospect of refloating the steamer, and so *The Brothers* took off 35 survivors with some difficulty and packed them into the lifeboat, while the remainder of the ship's crew took to their own boats and were towed to port by the Penzance steam drifter *Pioneer* (destined herself to be rescued by the Penlee Lifeboat in 1938). The well-earned rest of both lifeboats' crews following this service was disturbed in the night when reports came in that the abandoned *City Of Westminster* was sounding her siren. They both put to sea once more, only to find that the siren's lanyard had become caught in the rigging and was sounding the siren as the boat moved in the swells. The Runnelstone became her graveyard, as it has been to so many others.

The late 1920s and 1930s saw a considerable slackening in calls for the lifeboat's services. Between 1928 and 1935 only two services are recorded to Penlee's account. It was the common case for all the local lifeboats, and one can only guess at the cause. Certainly the age of steam - or more properly petrol and diesel oil - had solved the problem of the maritime trap, except in cases of engine breakdown. Fishing was in serious decline. Penzance's interest in fishing had reduced to next to nothing, and the beleaguered Newlyn fleet was forced to spend several months a year away on the east coast to make ends meet. The mighty shoals of pilchards had abandoned the waters around Lands End, never to return in numbers. On land nearly all the mines had failed. The whole country was in the grip of a recession which affected the volume of all businesses, shipping included. Many of Penzance's old established industries did not survive the slump. But perhaps the most significant factor was the improvement in land transport, where roads and a very efficient rail freight service could carry goods between one part of the country and another in hours, rather than the days still required for sea voyages. Boating for leisure was still almost unknown in the far west. The overall volume of shipping visiting Mounts Bay thus declined to probably its lowest level since records began.

However there was a very significant event in the history of Penlee. Thanks to legacies from Miss Coode of Launceston and Miss Young of Twickenham, *The Brothers* retired in 1931, to be replaced by a new twin-engine twin-screw Watson class. The donors wished to honour two relatives, Winifred Coode and Sidney Webb, but spared the station the burden of the full names, and settled for the initials *W & S*.

Preparing to re-house the *W & S*. (RNLI archive).

The *W & S* was a beautiful boat, handsome to look at and sturdy in design. She made no concessions to the pulling and sailing past except for a small mizzen, and was the model of lifeboats up until the late 1970s. Her engines were not exposed as *The Brothers'* had been, but set in an engine room with a funnel and ventilators, as on larger boats. She also had covered quarters for the survivors, an unheard-of luxury. *W & S* was destined to become the longest-serving lifeboat in the station's records, on station from 1931 to 1960, and is still (at the time of writing) enjoying an active career as a leisure craft.

CHAPTER 8

Within three weeks *W & S* was needed by the steamship *Opal* which had suffered a severe cargo shift off Lands End. A coaster was on hand and managed to rescue ten crew in very heavy seas, but by the time the Penlee and Sennen boats arrived there remained only the melancholy task of searching for bodies. The *W & S* recovered the body of the captain, who had been washed clean off the steamer's bridge.

Gradually the tempo of rescues began to pick up, and one stood out as a classic of old. In 1936 in typical 'lifeboat weather', ie 2am on a freezing January night in a SSW gale, with heavy seas and lashing rain, a boat was reported on fire near the Gear Rock off Penzance. It was the steamship *Taycraig*, and she was not on fire but had certainly struck the Gear Rock, the crew burning a mattress as a distress signal. The *Taycraig* was caught aft and was stern-on to the waves, so the lifeboat could enjoy no lee shelter in her approach. *W & S* under coxswain Frank Blewett, grappled her starboard side and hung grimly on, receiving a severe pounding and in frequent danger of being washed onto the steamer's decks. When the alignment of the two boats allowed, the crew jumped one by one, the ninth and last falling into the sea but scooped out alive by the lifeboat's crew. *W & S* arrived in Penzance at 3.25am. Later it was revealed that one of the lifeboat's engines had failed and she had carried out the rescue on half-power. It was one of Penlee's bravest services of the 20th century, and was properly rewarded by a Bronze Medal for Coxswain Blewett.

The *Taycraig*. (D Blewett collection).

With a revival of fishing and increasing international tension the volume of local shipping began to increase, and several rescues were carried out in the run-up to war. The most notable was the oddest. In the small hours of a January morning in 1939, the crew of the Ostend trawler *Paul Therese* were so exhausted that they did not notice when she slipped her moorings in Newlyn harbour, somehow drifted safely through the gaps, and began to drive across Mounts Bay in a SW gale. Luckily there are eyes awake in Newlyn at all hours, and her strange departure had been spotted. By the time the *W & S* caught up with her she was dangerously close to the rocks near St Michaels Mount. A lifeboatman jumped aboard and went below to rouse the still-sleeping crew. He fixed a tow to clear the immediate danger until the startled crew managed to start the engines and steam out of trouble. Prompt action had turned a near tragedy to comedy.

There was nothing comic about the service of 23rd January 1939, when the *W & S* was called in a desperate attempt to assist the St Ives lifeboat *John & Sarah Eliza Stych* which had been seen to overturn in St Ives Bay. Sennen Cove were unable to launch, and the *W & S* had actually negotiated Lands End before being recalled. The battering she had received had damaged her radio, and so a rocket was fired from Cape Cornwall to recall her, there sadly being no reason for her to proceed any further. All but one of the St Ives crew were lost.

The war made new and old demands on the local RNLI stations. There were many new fishing boats to care for, refugees from France and Belgium, whose lack of knowledge of the unfamiliar coast sometimes led them into trouble. There were calls to torpedoed vessels, missing aircraft, drifting life-rafts and ships' boats, and other casualties of war. *W & S* once even found herself standing by during a depth-charging operation off The Lizard in case the crew of the damaged U-boat should need rescuing. The crew of U-boat 1209 actually did need rescuing when she struck a more fearsome underwater object than herself and was wrecked on the Wolf Rock.

One of the most praiseworthy was not the most spectacular, to the Norwegian steamship *Heire*, which had lost a propeller off Lands End and was awaiting a tug. Sennen lifeboat had attended her earlier but had returned to station. The *Heire's* position became dangerous, but Sennen were unable to re-launch because of the conditions, so *W & S* set off at midnight of 2nd February 1941 to stand by her, keeping close by in freezing conditions and a NE gale until the next morning when the tug arrived and the tow was safely established, returning home after twelve bitter hours at sea.

In a record-breaking incident, *W & S* landed the fine total of 57 survivors from the frigate HMS *Teme* which had been torpedoed and was being towed in by a naval tug. After breaking the tow rope in freshening conditions, the Navy requested the lifeboat to land the 57, who, having been rescued once already did not count as an official lifeboat rescue, through they must have made an impressive crush aboard. The records note that they were kept happy with 'biscuits and rum'.

A significant service took place immediately after the war, although it did not seem so at the time. The yacht *Diane* was bound from Cowes to the Mediterranean, and very nice too, when she began to drag ashore in SSW gale off Newlyn and lost an anchor. *W & S* obliged by passing a line in the rough and shallow water and towing her into Newlyn, the first pleasure craft to be rescued by Penlee, the fore-runner of a seemingly endless line.

The battleship HMS *Warspite*. (D Blewett collection).

And then, in April 1947, there was HMS *Warspite*.

The grand old battleship was on her final voyage from Portsmouth to the breakers' yards on the Clyde towed by two tugs, with a passage crew of eight aboard. Penlee had already been alerted by a scare as she first attempted to pass Lands End, but did not need to launch. Later came the message that she had broken away from her tugs and was drifting freely across Mounts Bay in a strong SW gale. At low water she grounded on a ledge off Cudden Point, and the *W & S* was soon in attendance, advising the master to abandon ship before the tide refloated her and cast her further ashore. The master thought little of their chances of transferring to the lifeboat in such seas and refused. *W & S* returned to Newlyn to await developments. After an hour the news came through that the *Warspite* had indeed refloated and was driving onto the rocks. The lifeboat launched once more into worsening conditions and very rough seas, taking a hour to reach the battleship, which was now in a desperate position, hard aground with head to sea and being swept by breaking waves. Coxswain Edwin Madron, on his first service as Cox, took the lifeboat to windward and then turned down towards her...

"30ft waves were coming down on her. All round was heavy broken water. Her starboard side was close to shore. Off her port side and at her stern the Cox could see rocks appearing in the troughs of the seas. But between the warship and the rocks was a channel some 40 yards wide. They took the lifeboat down this channel, pumping oil as they went. ...They could have found some shelter near the stern, but a boat was slung in davits outboard. He chose a spot at the far end of the quarter-deck, turned, and brought the lifeboat in, head to wind. In a momentary lull he threw two lines aboard. Then began the perilous task of holding the lifeboat close enough for the men to jump in. One moment they looked down on the warship's deck, and the next they were in grave danger of being smashed on a bulge below her waterline. Watching each sea the Cox went full

speed ahead to meet it and then full speed astern. For 35 minutes he manoeuvred in this way and whenever the lifeboat swung close enough he called upon the men one by one to jump. Seven jumped as soon as they were called, but the eighth took a long time before he dared. Throughout the two mechanics were crouched under the canopy at the controls, unable to see what was going on, but well aware that the slightest delay in carrying out the coxswain's instructions could mean disaster for all."

RNLI Lifeboat Journal

The rescue was witnessed by a huge crowd on shore who watched appalled as time after time the lifeboat seemed doomed to founder, especially during the long wait for the last man.

It was the most celebrated rescue since the *Saluto,* recorded in newsreel and photographs and breathless accounts in the national newspapers. The RNLI responded with a Silver Medal for Edwin Madron, a Bronze Medal for Mechanic Johnny Drew, and Thanks on Vellum to Second Coxswain Joe Madron, Bowman Jack Worth, Assistant Mechanic Jack Wallis and Crewmen Abraham Madron, Ben Jeffery, and Clarry Williams. The *Warspite* was later briefly refloated and beached beside St Michaels Mount, where she became part of the scenery for several years as she was slowly broken up on the sands.

Edwin Madron photographed after the *Warspite* rescue.
(Janet Madron collection).

Many notable rescues awaited the *W & S* but it was a relief lifeboat *Millie Walton* which returned to the scene of the *Warspite* rescue at Cudden Point in 1956, in aid of the steamer *Yewcroft.* In dense fog the *Yewcroft* had reported that she had gone ashore "position unknown but think near the Brisons" The steamer was aground bow and stern though unsupported in the centre, and as the tide fell she broke apart so suddenly that it sounded like a gunshot. Apart from the Chief Engineer who was trapped on the after section and had to be rescued by Breeches Buoy, the lifeboat rescued all 10 of the remaining, disoriented crew, after having gone aground herself near the Mount on the way.

There were sadder calls, in particular to the French trawler *Vert Prairial*, who managed to get off a brief SOS before going ashore near Porthcurno, leaving only the melancholy task of recovering the bodies of her crew of 17 from the surf.

The *Vert Prairial*, Porthcurno. (D Blewett collection).

Medicos were also becoming part of the regular routine, while more unusual services included landing keepers from lighthouses and light-ships, and standing by a seaplane which had landed to seek survivors from a crashed aeroplane. The seaplane was unable to take off and the *W & S* shadowed her as she taxied slowly across Mounts Bay until taken in tow off The Lizard by an RAF rescue launch. Helicopters too were playing their part, the first combined rescue taking place off the Wolf in 1948.

In 1957 there was a more personal occasion, as Mr Barrie Bennetts was awarded the RNLI's highest honour to a voluntary worker, that of Honorary Life Governor, after serving as Penlee's Honorary Secretary for 44 years.

W & S too was becoming a veteran, and in 1960 a state-of-the-art Watson class was finally scheduled to replace her. On June 15th the MV *Rowallan Castle* requested medical attention and called into Mounts Bay so that *W & S* could land an injured man. It was her last service before making way for the brand-new *Solomon Browne*.

CHAPTER 9

Solomon Browne was another large step up the evolutionary ladder of lifeboats. Although her hull design was fundamentally little different from the old gigs and whalers of olden times, she was completely enclosed above. Even the central cockpit steering position could be closed in poor conditions. Behind it was a cabin with space for navigational equipment and aids, where both radar and Decca were later added. Below was a forward cabin for survivors, and the engine room.

The engines were two Gardner 60hp diesels, powering twin screws in protective tunnels, a reliable power-pack which kept her going at a steady nine knots in all conditions. The hull was wooden, of double-diagonal mahogany planking with canvas sheeting glued between, robust enough for the closest of encounters. Her vital statistics were 47' long by 13' beam, fairly filling the Penlee boathouse, with a weight of 22 tons.

Her price was also of another order of magnitude. The major factor towards her £35,500 cost was a legacy from Miss Lydia Mary Dyer Browne of Launceston, who requested that the lifeboat be named after her father, a squire and gentleman farmer from Landrake. Legacies from Miss Waterhouse of Huddersfield and Miss Davies of Cheshire contributed also, the balance being made up from RNLI funds. On 17th September 1960 she was officially named in Mousehole harbour by Lady Tedder.

Mousehole crowded for the naming ceremony of the *Solomon Browne*, September 1960. (Jim Hodge collection).

Her first service was of almost poetic gentleness, to take off a mother and her new-born baby from the MV *Fravizo* in the calm waters of Gwavas Lake early on a quiet September morning.

RNAS Culdrose was still flying Fairy Gannets and Buccaneer jets, and its days as a mainly helicopter base were still in the future. So, with improved radio communications, *Solomon Browne* took responsibility for most medicos in the western approaches, as her record shows. She performed no less than thirteen of these in her first full year, mostly employing the medical services of the redoubtable Dr Dennis Leslie who later became Chairman of the Penlee Branch.

Solomon Browne's crew returning from night service.
(Janet Madron collection).

It came almost as a rude shock when a real emergency arose, the trawler *Jeanne Gougy*, which had ploughed into the Armed Knight off Lands End in appalling conditions in November 1962. The original response was made by the reserve lifeboat *Edmund & Mary Robinson* from Sennen and by helicopter, but the trawler was being swamped on her side hard against the rocks, unreachable by sea, and the only service they could give was to recover bodies. However, even as a TV crew were filming the battered wreck, an arm suddenly appeared from the wheelhouse, waving for help. The cliff rescue team managed to get a line aboard and pulled six survivors from the wheelhouse where an air pocket had saved them. This gave new heart to the rescuers and the *Solomon Browne* was quickly sent for, but her searches found no more of the crew of 18 alive.

Another tragedy unfolded in October 1963. At 3am on the 23rd the Spanish coaster *Juan Ferrer* managed to get off only the chillingly vague message "Aground in the vicinity of Lands End..." before going off air. Searchers at Boscawen Point picked out wreckage at sea with their torches, and made out a figure clinging to it. It was the captain, Luiz Ignacio Ruiz, who was quickly rescued by the *Solomon Browne*. Three other survivors were found walking down a farm lane at Tregiffian, having clambered ashore, but the rest of the crew of fifteen were dead. The wreck led to the building of a new lighthouse below Tregiffian, at Tater Dhu.

Tragedy had visited even closer to home. In 1961 while rehousing from a routine medico, a sudden heavy sea swept the lifeboat sideways from the Penlee slipway. The lifeboat was unharmed, but the winch wire which was attached to her caught the legs of two of the slip crew and knocked them off the side, onto the rocks below. Mr R W Blewett was rescued with no more than broken ribs, but Mr James Pentreath tumbled onto the rocks and into the water, and was found to be dead on recovery. It was a sad end to a long record of good fortune, for the extraordinary fact was that, despite over 150 years of desperately dangerous endeavour, it was the station's first fatality.

In all *Solomon Browne* is recorded as having performed 79 medicos, causing many people from professional sailors to inexperienced passengers to be grateful for her skill. The mackerel fishery had also grown, encouraging many small fishing vessels to try their luck from Newlyn, some of whom inevitably came to grief with engine failure and other troubles. She remained busy.

Vicar of Paul Rev Cadman conducts blessing of *Solomon Browne* at high tide in Mousehole harbour. (H G Welby collection).

Two highly newsworthy occasions involved the *Solomon Browne*. The first was in March 1967 when she took over from the exhausted crew of the St Mary's lifeboat *Guy & Clare Hunter* on standby duty beside the colossal wreck of the oil tanker *Torrey Canyon* on the Seven Stones, paddling through the thick and stinking oil for 36 hours before returning home to the equally daunting task of cleaning her hull and topsides. Twelve years later she remained on standby for 48 hours as the disastrous outcome of the Fastnet Yacht Race unfolded, eventually being launched to recover the yacht *Gan*.

But the most extreme demand on the lifeboat and crew to date came on 25th January 1975.

Solomon Browne was called at 6.30am to make all speed to the MV *Lovat* which was reported sinking in terrible conditions 25 miles south of The Lizard. Even her coxswain, trawler skipper Trevelyan Richards, had never encountered such seas, but having heard that there were men in the water - including a helicopter winchman whose line had broken - he kept up a speed of 9 knots in the WNW gales which were gusting to hurricane force. On scene the waves were so high as to make helicopter operations almost impossible. *Solomon Browne*, despite a roll of up to 60 degrees, managed to secure a liferaft alongside and recover the two crewmen from it, but both were dead, one a boy of no more than 16. She searched the scene, guided by the helicopters, and recovered a further three bodies from the water. It was harrowing for all the crew, and especially for Stephen Madron who had spent time with the *Lovat's* crew a few days earlier in Cardiff. Eventually it was reported that all her complement were accounted for, and *Solomon Browne* set off for home through breaking seas of up to 40-50 feet. The RNLI rewarded her efforts, with a Bronze Medal for Trevelyan Richards, and Thanks on Vellum to Second Cox Frank Wallis, Bowman Phil Wallis, Mechanic Nigel Brockman, Asst Mechanic Stephen Madron, and crewmen Alan Tregenza, Barry Torrie, and young Kevin Smith.

More and more of *Solomon Browne's* customers were pleasure craft, yachts, catamarans and motor boats, as well as the regular fishing fleet. In March 1980 the Belgian trawler *Normauwil* failed (not for the last time) to make the gaps into Newlyn in a strong SE wind and quickly grounded. *Solomon Browne* was forced to go into the shallowest water in a heavy sea to pass her a tow, grounding once or twice on the way, but succeeded in keeping the trawler's head up to the wind until the tide allowed her to be pulled clear. Trevelyan Richards received a framed letter of thanks from the Chairman of the RNLI for his seamanship and determination.

Photo call following the *Lovat* service, l to r - David Brown, Kevin Smith, Stephen Madron, Trevelyan Richards, Nigel Brockman, Leslie Nicholls, Mark Johansen, Ruel Schaap. (Janet Madron collection).

On 8th December 1981 *Solomon Browne* had a shout to assist the FV *Quo Vadis*. On 18th December many of the crew were present at the switch-on of the annual Mousehole Christmas Lights. Crewman John Blewett, an electrician, was a leading helper in the erection of the famous displays. The honour of switching on the lights went to crewman Charlie Greenhaugh, the landlord of the Ship Inn. It was a cold, clear and still night, and the sound of the carols and the accompanying brass band echoed around the hills above the village.

Solomon Browne's crew line up to meet the Queen at opening of Mary Williams pier in Newlyn, 1980. (Andrew Besley).

CHAPTER 10

The wind rose in the morning of 19th December and strengthened all day. By nightfall a full southerly gale was blowing, with a forecast of a storm force 10 to come. It was the last Saturday before Christmas, and spirits were not dampened by the bad weather, though the coloured lights in the narrow streets tugged at their supports. However in a few homes news was arriving which might affect the evening's plans. Shortly after 6pm Trevelyan Richards received a telephone call from Falmouth Coastguard Station, informing him that the coaster *Union Star* had reported an engine breakdown six miles east of the Wolf Rock. This put her to the south of the granite coast of West Penwith, in danger - as with any sailing ship of old - of driving onto a lee shore. The call was advisory only, since there appeared to be time to see if the coaster, on her maiden voyage, could sort her problems out unaided. RNAS Culdrose was preparing a helicopter, and a tug on station in Mounts Bay had also been informed.

Falmouth Coastguard Station was a new institution. Having given the message they expected that the lifeboat crew would muster at the boathouse and wait for the call or the stand-down. However Penlee boathouse was not a place to encourage a long wait for the crew. *Solomon Browne* almost filled it up, and with no facilities other than a small brass stove, it was cold and cramped. Instead the crew were used to being contacted by telephone and waiting at home for the signal to go. Trevelyan rang Mechanic Stephen Madron and Second Mechanic Nigel Brockman. The word went round.

For the next hour and a half, nothing happened at all. Trevelyan had his tea and took out his charts. Few seamen knew that area of coastline better than he did, but there are rocks and shoals which have to be paid attention at different states of the tide, especially in such a gale.

Elsewhere the drama of the *Union Star* was being played out. The tug *Noord Holland* was already under way and had passed Mousehole in 15-20' seas which her skipper Guy Buurman later described as " ... for the combination of size and steepness, the worst I have seen". The helicopter had been made ready and was crossing Mounts Bay to make visual contact with the *Union Star*, and to take off the master's wife and two teenage step-children as he had requested. Despite the local conditions there was no particular panic, and the *Union Star's* skipper seemed convinced that he was drifting only slowly towards the land.

However as soon as the helicopter confirmed the radar reports from Lands End regarding the *Union Star's* true position, time was suddenly very short. She was seen to be only two miles from the point of Tater Dhu, and driving before the storm. Falmouth Coastguards rang Trevelyan and requested an immediate launch. As was his custom Trevelyan left his mother Mary to call out the crew while he left for the lifeboat station. She rang the crew and the launching crew, and when she heard the signal maroons above the noise of the storm, her task was done, and she settled down to wait as many times before. Trevelyan had swept out in a hurry and "...the door slammed behind him with the wind"

In the boathouse at Penlee the normal drill of a launch was soon taking place. The doors were opened and the fury of the storm roared around the boathouse. Most of the regular crew were soon aboard, but there was still room for a volunteer. Several men offered their services but were refused. Nigel Brockman's young son Neil put himself forward, but Trevelyan turned him down also, sobering the assembly by saying "No more than one from a family on a night like this". Then Charlie Greenhaugh, landlord of the Ship Inn and veteran of the Royal Navy and merchant navy appeared, and Trevelyan smilingly motioned him on board.

The rise and fall of the water was so extreme that the launch had to be carefully timed, in order to avoid being knocked off the slipway or caught at the bottom. Just after 8.15pm Trevelyan gave the signal to knock out the retaining pin, and the *Solomon Browne* began to slide down the slipway, chasing a retreating wave. She made a perfect launch, and set course for Tater Dhu.

It took the lifeboat half an hour to make the 2½ mile journey, constantly on her beam ends, battered and swept by the fierce seas. On scene she met a desperate, frustrating situation. *Union Star* was drifting into a shallow bay, bounded by Tater Dhu to the east and Boscawen Point to the west, with precious little sea-room left. The tug had already concluded that there was no safe way to establish a tow so close to shore, particularly since the *Union Star* was by now anchored by the bow. She was standing off to observe. The Sea King helicopter had spent an hour trying to pass a line to the coaster, being unable to put a man aboard because of the wild whipping of her mast in seas now rising to 30-40'. Nothing seemed to work, and, despite being called late to the scene, it seemed that only the lifeboat could give practical assistance. Trevelyan offered his services : "..Do you want for us to come alongside and take the woman and children?" Mick Moreton, *Union Star's* captain, replied politely that he would be much obliged.

As with the *Taycraig* and the *Warspite*, the casualty was head-to-wind and could give the lifeboat no working lee. Trevelyan brought the *Solomon Browne* in as gently as he could to the coaster's side, and made a heavy contact while the deck crew threw lines over her rail in order to hold on for a few seconds while the crew transferred. But no-one came out of the *Union Star's* wheelhouse, and after a few moments the lifeboat was forced to disengage and come round again. The manoeuvre was repeated and repeated. The five agile crew members might have successfully made the dash for the *Solomon Browne*, but the captain's wife and two teenage stepdaughters were also aboard, by now cold, tired and terrified. It was stalemate.

Trevelyan changed tactics and veered down using the drogue, or sea-anchor. They were so close to shore that the wave patterns were becoming unpredictable, likely to arise from any quarter. The vessels collided time after time with great force, but the Watson was designed for such encounters. Above the helicopter was making a last desperate attempt to land a winchman, breaking off only when thrown violently back through the air towards the cliff. The whipping ship's mast had missed her rotors by as little as 3'. The two vessels drove towards the breakers, only a couple of hundred yards from the shore in seas beyond anyone's experience. But still none of the *Union Star's* crew came out.

The impasse was broken when the *Union Star's* anchor chain parted, and she swerved broadside to the sea. Although she was barely 50 yards from shore, still the *Solomon Browne* pursued her. On her second approach a huge wave threw her up into the air and smashed her down on top of the *Union Star's* hatches, all her keel visible. The coaster rolled, and the lifeboat slid backwards into the water. The watchers in the helicopter thought she was bound to founder. But instead they saw to their astonishment that she was still under control and making yet another pass towards the *Union Star*. Later the helicopter pilot, Lt-Commander Russell Smith of the US Navy described the lifeboat crew as "the bravest eight men" and called their actions in returning to the casualty after being beached on her hatches as "the greatest act of courage I have ever seen."

The *Union Star's* complement finally threw all caution to the winds and rushed down to the lower decks. A wave buried them, but as it cleared the *Solomon Browne* was alongside, and four casualties were quickly snatched aboard. One or two more appeared to be in the water. *Solomon Browne* stood off for a moment and radioed in that "We've got four off at the moment, male and female. There's two left on board...".

With an inexplicable noise, communications suddenly ceased.

But the lifeboat was still afloat. The helicopter pilot's last view of her before he turned for home was heading seawards immediately after the rescue to avoid the breakers, and making a starboard turn. Guy Buurman on the tug *Noord Holland* was standing off in deeper water. His last view of her was high on a wave silhouetted by the *Union Star's* lights just before the coaster finally struck the shore and overturned. Ashore the cliff rescue party was still struggling down into position.

Suddenly there were no witnesses.

Falmouth Coastguards called the lifeboat to acknowledge the news of the rescue and asked for further information. There was no reply. The Coastguards called again and again, but the airwaves were silent. The cliff rescue party arrived a few minutes later, but saw only the wreck of the *Union Star*, and an otherwise empty sea. There was no sign of the *Solomon Browne*.

CHAPTER 11

Andrew Besley

It was unthinkable. It was part of a lifeboat's natural pattern that she went out in whatever conditions prevailed, performed a rescue if at all possible, and returned to station with all hands. That was the way it always was, and always had been. Nothing else made sense.

Coastguard Don Buckfield was lowered down on a harness to a small cleft behind the upturned coaster. There appeared to be a lifeboatman's lifejacket loose in the surf, but he was unable to reach it.

The silence from the *Solomon Browne* was becoming unbearable. Shore parties called out for her on mobile radios, the rescue helicopter returned to search and call for her in what were now hurricane conditions, and fishermen called from the radios on their boats. Then rumours began to spread of lifeboat wreckage coming ashore amongst the pounding breakers in Lamorna Cove. Soon there could be no doubt. The unthinkable was true.

It was essential to explore the remotest possibility that somehow, somewhere at sea survivors might be clinging to rafts or wreckage, and the RNLI gave orders to launch lifeboats from all the flank stations, Sennen, The Lizard and even St Mary's. Sennen were quite unable to pass Lands End and had to return to station. St Mary's on the other hand came with the wind, which had veered towards the westerly. Their brand new Arun class, *Robert Edgar* arrived on scene in less than two hours. The Lizard lifeboat,

Duke Of Cornwall had the worst of it, beating into the teeth of the storm all the way across the exposed waters of Mounts Bay, and incidentally suffering such structural damage that she had to be taken out of service immediately afterwards.

But by now the search was for wreckage and bodies, not survivors, and they all knew it. At about 9.25 pm all eight casualties from the *Union Star* had perished, and with them the eight crew from Mousehole, almost certainly overwhelmed by the huge seas in a last desperate attempt to reach the "two left on board…".

No-one slept that night. The news was not confirmed on the BBC until the next morning, but those who already knew were numbed by shock and grief. The streets of Mousehole were full of people going from one house to another, to comfort each other, talk or just sit silently together. It was too terrible to grasp.

The officers and committee of Penlee Branch were doing their best to cope with the circumstances. There were the immediate arrangements to make, decisions to take regarding the families, the disposal of the wreckage, the accommodation of the personnel already heading westwards, the desire of others to help, the messages of sympathy, the huge and growing demands of the news media. They tried to think of everything, but Honorary Secretary Del Johnson was floored on visiting Mousehole the following morning. He was met by a deputation of local men wanting to know how soon a relief lifeboat could be brought to Penlee, and volunteering to man it. Who knew when her services might be needed again? The men were adamant. You couldn't have a lifeboat station without a lifeboat. Even as they were speaking, fishing boats, lifeboats and helicopters were sweeping the seas outside the harbour walls, searching for the bodies of their friends and companions. It only made their resolve stronger. It was a response in the great traditions of the RNLI, typical of lifeboatmen everywhere.

The RNLI was already covering the operational side of the disaster. The *Duke of Cornwall* under coxswain Peter Mitchell and *Robert Edgar* under coxswain Matt Lethbridge spent a grim day recovering wreckage, and were finally sent on their long journeys home as night fell. A 70' relief Clyde class slipped into Newlyn to cover immediate eventualities. Within a few days there was a meeting in the Seamen's Mission at Newlyn for all potential volunteers for a new Penlee crew. While grief and mourning, fund-raising, funerals, inquests, and often deeply intrusive press attention went on all around them, the remaining core of the Penlee station went about the business of trying to revive it as an effective rescue unit.

The nightmare went on, over Christmas and New Year. Only four of the *Union Star's* complement were found, and only four of the crew of the *Solomon Browne* came back to shore, Trevelyan Richards, Nigel Brockman, John Blewett and Charlie Greenhaugh. The others: Stephen Madron, Barrie Torrie, Gary Wallis and Kevin Smith, were never recovered.

As well as the individual funerals, a local memorial service for the whole crew was held in Paul Church at the end of January, attended by the Duke and Duchess of Kent. A larger memorial service was held in Truro Cathedral in February, attended by the Duke of Atholl and the Prime Minister, Mrs Thatcher.

The lost crew were duly honoured by the RNLI. Trevelyan Richards was posthumously awarded their highest accolade, a Gold Medal, and the seven crew were each awarded the Bronze Medal. In May 1982 the awards were received by the eight families at a ceremony in the Royal Festival Hall.

William Trevelyan Richards   James Stephen Madron

Nigel Brockman   John Robert Blewett   Charles Thomas Greenhaugh

Kevin Smith   Barrie Robertson Torrie   Gary Lee Wallis

The crew of the *Solomon Browne*. These photographs are still exhibited in the old Penlee Boathouse.

The inquest was held, and a public enquiry was scheduled, although it did not begin sitting until March 1983. The eight families endured an ongoing ordeal, firstly from bereavement, then by the constant interest of the media. Penlee was no longer a relatively obscure lifeboat station but suddenly the most famous in the country, and known throughout the world. The everyday actions of lifeboat stations, however spectacular and successful, usually attracted only short-lived public attention. But the loss of a whole crew, from a well-visited, attractive village, threw the public spotlight on the work of the lifeboat service as a whole, they risks they regularly take, and the instincts which inspire them. "Penlee" became a media 'buzz-word', and any story relating to it was sure of extensive coverage. Anniversaries of the disaster and any other news of Penlee aroused widespread public interest, and still do. Penlee became public property. In many, many ways things were never the same.

The *Solomon Browne* was commemorated locally in several locations, amongst them the dedication of a Memorial Garden adjacent to the boathouse, opened in 1985.

In the meantime, the wishes of the new volunteers had to be addressed and the re-establishment of Penlee as a lifeboat station given priority. It was an unfamiliar situation for all concerned, at local level and headquarters alike, although sadly not unprecedented. Two Cornish lifeboats and crews had already been lost in the 20th century, the Padstow steam lifeboat *James Stevens* in 1900 and the St Ives lifeboat *John & Sarah Eliza Stych*, as already mentioned, in 1939.

Guy & Clare Hunter 1982. (Roy Pascoe collection).

The normal evolution of a station means that young or inexperienced members join a core of fully experienced and skilled crew, familiar with the technology, practice and procedures, local conditions, and every aspect of running a lifeboat. Though there were a number of volunteers available who had served a long and valuable turn on the *Solomon Browne*, the line of continuity had been broken. The RNLI set about restoring this deficiency as soon as possible. A relief Watson *Charles Henry Ashley* replaced the Clyde for a short while, but the longer-term replacement was a lifeboat well-known to all at Penlee, *Guy & Clare Hunter*, another Watson, which had served at St Mary's, Isles of Scilly magnificently from 1956 until its recent replacement by the *Robert Edgar*.

With her came RNLI temporary staff Coxswain, Tam Beattie, who took over the leadership of the local team, with the assistance of staff mechanic, John Leech. The new crew were eager to learn, and with *Guy & Clare Hunter* had a boat almost identical to *Solomon Browne*. By February 1982 new officers had been appointed. Kenny Thomas from Newlyn had been chosen as Coxswain, with Les Nicholls as Second Coxswain, Roydon Paynter as Reserve Coxswain, Mike Inskip as Mechanic and Bobby Keates as Second Mechanic, and a good pool of available crewmen, both young and older. Penlee was inspected and declared fully operational. The loss of the former crew was a wound which could never be healed, but the station lived again, and this helped to divert the enduring grief into action.

The first test of the new crew came on 14th April 1882, rescuing the FV *Halcyon* and her two crew. There were several other shouts during the year, including the rescue of a punt and its two occupants in September. April 1983 saw three significant services: the first to help evacuate the large passenger ferry *Armorique* which came into the bay after a fire, 38 of her passengers being packed into the Watson's limited space; the second on the same day, when the first ever service to wind-surfers in difficulties took place: and the third was a notable escort to the MV *Wilgo* which was limping across the bay from Porthleven under reduced power in a Force 9 gale.

And with that (apart from a brief shout as a relief lifeboat in July) the *Guy & Clare Hunter* went back into the reserve fleet. The loss of the *Solomon Browne* had in fact marked the end of another era at Penlee, and a fresh page was about to be printed in its long history. At 00.01 on Sunday 8th May 1983, the new Arun Class *Mabel Alice*, identification No 52-24, went into service, and after 70 years the station moved back once again to Newlyn.

*For a fuller account of the disaster, read "Penlee - The Loss of a Lifeboat" by the same author, published by Truran, now in its third (2005) edition.

First line-up of the new crew, 1982, l to r - (Standing) Roy Pascoe, Phil Wallis, Leslie Nicholls, Kenny Thomas, Mike Inskip, Bobby Keates, Roydon Paynter. (Kneeling) Edwin Madron, Frank Wallis.

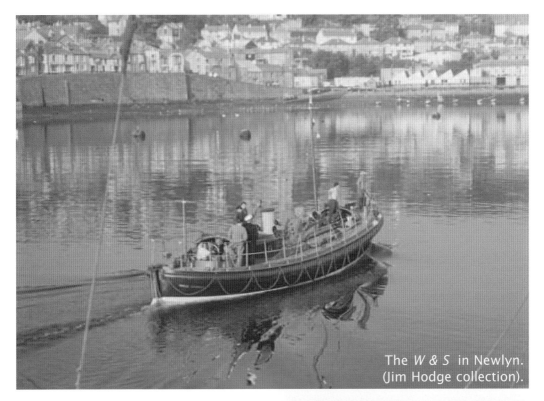

The *W & S* in Newlyn.
(Jim Hodge collection).

Messing around in boats –
Stephen Madron and
Charlie Greenhaugh
in Penlee boathouse.
(Roy Pascoe collection).

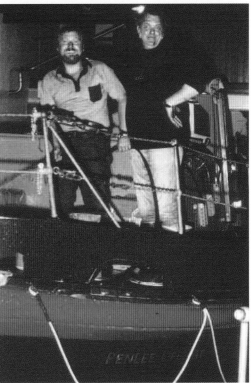

Trevelyan Richards.
(Janet Madron collection).

Nigel and Neil Brockman.
(Janet Madron collection).

Stephen Madron.
(Janet Madron collection).

(Penlee collection).

Wave-jumping
in the Y-boat.
(Roy Pascoe collection).

Four men and a wealth of
lifeboat experience –
Roy Pascoe, Bobby Keates,
Neil Brockman and
Joey Jeffery pose outside
the boathouse.
(Neil Brockman collection).

Lilies off the starboard bow –
one of many models of
Mabel Alice.
(Neil Brockman collection).

CREW LIST AND

Ben Keogh

Martin Wardle

Neil Brockman
(Coxswain)

Rob Cooke
(Tractor Driver)

Julia Rescorla-Ryan

Ralph Curnow
(Emergency Mechanic)

Dan Wardle

David Pascoe
(2nd Cox)

Jed Payne
(Third Mechanic)

Spencer Robertson

Zac Haining

Paul Ashworth

Patrick Harvey
(Full-time Mechanic/Dep 2nd Cox)

OFFICERS 2005

David Osborne
(ILB Mechanic)

Roy Pascoe
(Deputy Launching Authority)

Paul Carne

Jake Freethy
(Shore Crew)

Marc Drew

Richard Nicholls
(2nd Mechanic)

Michael Curnow

Steven Ashley

Tony Rendle

Paul Oliver

Andrew Munson
(Lifeboat Operations Manager)

Ian Neal

James Taylor

Cutting a dash – *Mabel Alice* on display. (Roy Pascoe collection).

Scalloper *Jacoba* high and dry
in Lamorna Cove. (M Sagar-Fenton).

Double gold -
Rosalie Johnson and mum
Binkie Wallen with their gold badges.
(Rosalie Johnson collection).

Cream teas on the prom
keep the boats afloat,
l to r -
Margaret Pascoe,
Eleanor Bushby,
Sue Collins,
Janet Madron.

Ivan Ellen passes Penlee boathouse. (Nicholas Leach).

2001
Calendar
boys.

Paul Alexander
wake-surfing.
(Nicholas Leach).

CHAPTER 12

The move was in itself a painful decision. Mousehole had just lost its lifeboat and eight of its sons, and the return to normal service at Penlee Point had helped to alleviate the grief. But the days of the old station had been numbered before the disaster. The Arun Class was not designed for slipway launching, but had to lie afloat at moorings at all states of the tide. The forward thrust of modernisation which had driven the RNLI throughout its existence could not stop for reasons of sentiment.

The new type of lifeboat was the most fundamental revolution in design since the days of Greathead. Until the late 1960s, lifeboats had grown in size, weight, superstructure, equipment and motive power, but the essential shape of the hull had not really altered since the days of sail, and the main construction was still of wood. The Watson Class was still designed to lie low and 'swim' through the weather, taking where necessary a considerable amount of sea on deck. The Arun Class was built to fly.

The basic design went back to wartime Air-Sea Rescue vessels and MTBs, large speedboats whose rapid propulsion lifted them out of the water as they went, cutting through the tops of waves rather than ploughing through the middle. They, and the American Coastguard vessel on which the initial trials were based, were made of metal, but as the technology of lighter fibre-glass (grp) developed, the RNLI became convinced that a boat could be built which would be fast enough to justify the wholesale change, while being durable enough to withstand the battering it was sure to receive.

Mabel Alice at Falmouth
Boat Construction,
Flushing.
(Roy Pascoe collection).

It looked like no lifeboat had ever looked, and naturally aroused considerable speculation and criticism. Its buoyancy and self-righting ability was based not on air-boxes or flotation compartments but mainly on the large watertight 'bubble' of the superstructure. Indeed the height of the bubble and the weight of the engines gave such force to the self-righting process that it had to be slowed down artificially with water chambers. Designers were discovering that they could design vessels to such high specifications that flesh-and-blood humans could not keep up, and the initial self-righting speed would have plastered the crew to the side of the cabin.

The superstructure gave the Arun its sit-up-and-beg stance, a large encompassing chamber within which all parts of the vessel could be accessed. It had a very useful 'flying bridge' on top, giving the coxswain a tremendous gain in all-round visibility, so important in close rescue situations. It also shipped a small inflatable dinghy, easily launched over the stern for close and shallow work, the 'Y - boat'. The men still had to be on deck during a rescue, but the journey to work became dryer than ever before in lifeboat history. The doubling in speed - from the Watson's 9 knots to the Arun's 18 - gave the crew other problems, in that it was not practical for them to wander about while racing through heavy weather as they had been accustomed to do. They would have been in more danger of injury than the casualties, and so they had to have specified passage stations, aircraft-style seats with safety belts. The boats were equipped with the latest in radio, radar , Decca, and other electronics. It had a small galley, and even a 'heads'.

The cost had also increased immensely, by a factor of ten from the *Solomon Browne*. A new Arun cost a cool £350,000. However, the huge impact of the disaster had led to a new appreciation of the risks and sacrifices regularly made by volunteer crews and the work of the RNLI in general, which was expressed in a large overall increase in voluntary contributions from the public. Following the disaster, the millionaire

PENLEE LIFEBOAT
RNLB "MABEL ALICE"

Photo: Spectrum Studio, Newlyn

the lifeboat will be named by
HRH THE DUKE OF KENT
President of the Royal National Lifeboat Institution
at Newlyn on Monday, 18th July, 1983, at 11.40 a.m.

46

philanthropist David Robinson, who had already made a number of anonymous donations to the RNLI, pledged the full cost of a new Arun for Penlee, asking only that it should be named after his wife.

Her first call came only two days after entering active service, a standard tow-in for the French FV *Rayon de Soleil* which had broken down off Tater-Dhu. The crew list was a typical mixture of the old and new : Coxswain Kenny Thomas, Edwin Madron, Mike Inskip, Bobby Keates, and brothers Frank & Phil Wallis.

On 18th July 1983 Newlyn's North Quay was thronged as a bright and gleaming *Mabel Alice* was officially named by the Duke of Kent and handed over to the safe-keeping of the station. All those present felt that despite the deep and grievous ache left by the loss of the *Solomon Browne*, a new day had dawned for Penlee.

Hail and farewell, 1982. (Roy Pascoe collection).

The re-stationing required more than just a new lifeboat. The berth chosen for her was just to the west of Newlyn's own latest addition, the central Mary Williams Pier. A deep channel was dredged to ensure that even on the lowest spring tide she would be able to answer the call without delay. The channel could not be dredged right up to the harbour infill or it would swiftly have blocked up again, so the lifeboat was moored about 50 metres offshore. To bridge the gap the crew hauled themselves to and fro on a small tender, sometimes being glad of their waterproofs even before a service had begun. A new boathouse was also constructed on the harbour car-park by the moorings, by permission of the Newlyn Harbour Commissioners. By the modern standards of the RNLI it was notable more for its economy than its beauty or luxury, but it was a vast improvement in facilities for those accustomed to the comforts of Penlee Point. It had a light and sunny assembly room, office, stores, toilet, and even a shower. It gave the station a focal point which - except possibly the Ship Inn - it had never previously enjoyed.

The old boathouse at Penlee Point was kept operational for several years afterwards, originally housing a relief Watson, looked after by some of the old Penlee launching crew including Raymond Pomeroy and Dudley Penrose. Even now, long after its official closure, it is still maintained in working order including the winch machinery, mainly by ex-crewman and now Deputy Launching Authority, Roy Pascoe. The old service boards decorate the walls, and a memorial to the lost crew - including their photographs - has pride of place. It is impossible to visit without imagining the colourful lifeboat with its chattering, laughing crew waiting to be hauled up the slipway after completing yet another mission.

The twenty-year service record of the *Mabel Alice* has not been previously published, and since it concerns many still active in the station, is recorded in full detail in Appendix 1. It provides a cross-section of the work of any modern lifeboat station, the variety, the hardship and occasional danger, upsetting and sad calls when lives could not be saved, calls which were pure farce, and many which were routine. It is unknown how many lives have been saved due to Penlee standard 'medicos' over the years, and it is virtually impossible to calculate how many millions of pounds-worth of shipping has been saved from destruction by a willing response and a steady tow, but it must be a great many.

It is also difficult to tell how many lives have been 'saved'. The RNLI has strict criteria on this, but they include only those plucked from imminent death. Good anticipation and a speedy response try to ensure wherever possible that rescues take place long before such extreme situations arise. Fixing a tow, passing a pump, transferring a crew member, supporting a helicopter rescue, escorting, advising, warning, simply being there - all these have saved lives in their turn by anticipating and preventing further danger, and the tally must amount to hundreds.

The following are just a few highlights of the *Mabel Alice's* 20-year career, to be found in full in the appendix:

- An epic tow of the French trawler *St Simeon* in February 1985, which also involved the Falmouth and Plymouth lifeboats, Penlee towing for nine hours in the teeth of a violent and freezing easterly storm, which earned the Thanks on Vellum for Kenny Thomas, and Certificates for the crew.

- A desperate but vain search for the four schoolboys swept off Lands End in May 1985, together with the Sennen lifeboat. Later a Sennen lifeboat was named the *Four Boys* in their memory.

- A service to yacht *Nasty* in August 1986, 25 miles SE of the station in a southerly gale, conditions on scene so rough that the two casualties had to be hauled through the water on lines moments before the yacht foundered.

- An unexpected encounter with 60' freak wave while on service west of Porthleven in October 1987, caught on video from the shore.

- An eerie repeat of the service to the *Paul Therese* in 1939, to Dutch yacht *Chinook* in June 1992, which was found to be drifting quietly out of the bay while her crew of three were asleep below.

48

- *Mabel Alice's* proudest hour: the service in December 1994, to the Newlyn crabber *Julian Paul* which had fouled her propeller 4 miles west of the Longships in a furious SW gale. Penlee attended together with Sennen lifeboat *Four Boys*, and towed for eight hours with Sennen escorting in winds up to Force 12, earning the RNLI Bronze Medal for Coxswain Neil Brockman and also for Coxswain Terry George of Sennen..

- Another terrific tow in October 1995 of the trawler *Ygraine*, a ten hour night service in gale force winds and rough seas, in which the tow parted twice.

- No less than four tow-ins between 1998 and 2000 of the vintage 1912 steam drifter *Feasible* which was vainly trying to make passage from Penzance to Bristol

- A display of previously unsuspected skills in September 1999 when successfully lassooing an unmanned runaway RIB in Penzance harbour.

- Possibly the most difficult and dangerous medico ever carried out by Penlee, in December 1999, to a seriously ill crewman from the French trawler *Gwel A Vo* in 15' seas, while the trawler was drifting broadside without power awaiting a tow, rewarded by Letter of Thanks from Chairman of RNLI

- A tricky rescue of four crew from MV *Dolfyn* just off Mousehole in December 2000, in rising seas and very shallow water.

- Falling into a "hole in the sea" at full speed en route to the Guernsey trawler *Chelaris J* in May 2002 in a force 9 SSE gale, slamming hard and causing damage to the lifeboat (relief Arun *City of Dublin*), then successfully towing in the casualty after a 9½ hour service.

But read them all...

After March 2001, *Mabel Alice* had company in Newlyn. After a routine coastal survey, the RNLI decided that the increasing leisure use of Mounts Bay required the services of an inshore lifeboat, for fast response and for use in shallow water. There had been a sub-station on St Michaels Mount since 1990, with a D-Class inflatable which had carried out valuable service, but it was felt that a larger Atlantic 75 RIB was needed, and that the best location would be adjacent to the existing station in Newlyn. A new boathouse was built and a relief Inshore Lifeboat (ILB) *City of Bradford IV* was brought in for trials.

The Atlantic was towed into the water by a submersible tractor, a delicate operation at low water as it involved tipping the trailer gingerly into the dredged channel without allowing the tractor to follow it down. It was originally demonstrated by an engineer named Kevin, and the name was soon transferred by driver Rob Cooke to the tractor itself. At every annual open-air lifeboat service, the station's chaplains still call for blessings for both lifeboats, and Kevin.

The Atlantic was an instant success, particularly on the 4th August 2001 when a series of fierce squalls fell on a bay full of swimmers, wind-surfers and racing dinghies, and she had to be everywhere at once. At the end of the summer the St Michaels Mount station closed, with the sadness every station closure brings, and the Penlee ILB was permanently established. In May 2003 a brand-new Atlantic was presented to Penlee by the family of the late Paul Alexander, after whom it was named.

It was not the only innovation. In January *Mabel Alice* performed her final service. She had arrived as a desperately-needed symbol of hope in Penlee's darkest hour, and a whole generation of crewmen and women had grown up on her, knowing no other boat. Her parting was an emotional moment, making a last dash up the coast to give a final salute to Mousehole, before speeding off to retirement. A relief Arun covered the station until 12th March, when a crowd of supporters turned out to welcome in the latest chapter in Penlee's story, the Severn Class *Ivan Ellen*

Farewell (Roy Pascoe collection).

CHAPTER 13

The Severn was not - like the Arun - a revolution in style, but was certainly an eye-popping development in size and sophistication. Visitors who look over *Ivan Ellen* are sometimes surprised to learn that she cost £1.8 million, but after a short tour they are surprised no longer. The range of electronic equipment would not look out of place on a jumbo-jet, much of it with user-friendly visuals showing the coxswain exactly where he is going, how fast, the shape of the coastline and underwater shoals, the depth of water, and what vessels or other obstructions stand in his way. Radio, radar, satellite all help to keep the information continuously updated, and CCTV gives him all-round vision without moving from the internal steering position. The seats have been upgraded again with hi-tech hydraulics to enable the crew to stand the impact of a high-speed dash through heavy seas without suffering internal injury.

The twin engines develop 2,500 bhp, (approximately the same power as the RMV *Scillonian*), with a throaty roar which propels her at a top speed of 25knots. The *Elizabeth & Blanche II* was Penlee's lifeboat within living memory (and is still afloat as a pleasure-boat), and had a power-pack of 15 strong men and a top speed of about 4 knots. *Ivan Ellen* is 10' longer, more significantly 10' wider, is 8 times as heavy, and cost 2,000 times as much. Every generation of lifeboats seems to have reached a plateau, beyond which further development seems pointless, although the RNLI is determined never to stand still, and the Severn's successor is already being tested in prototype. However it likely that she is the ultimate expression of a certain line of design, destined to be a classic. She is, as they say, 'some boat'.

Nicholas Leach

The Atlantic 75 too is only one in a continuing line of evolutionary vessels, but is certainly an impressive and effective lifeboat. Designed to get there fast in inshore and shallow water, she is the ideal response to the increasing use of the sea as a playground, serving yachts and pleasure-boats, surfers, windsurfers, kite-surfers, jet-skiers and swimmers, and also able to tow in larger craft in favourable conditions. In cases of drowning, hypothermia, heat-stroke etc, literally every second counts, and the Atlantic 75 with its three crew can launch in a few minutes and race to a casualty at up to 32 knots. It is hard to imagine how Mounts Bay ever managed without one.

In 2003, two hundred years after Penzance's first generous impulse for the provision of a purpose-built lifeboat, three ceremonies took place.

The first was the formal naming of the *Paul Alexander*, handed over by Paul's stepfather Richard to the RNLI deputy Chairman Sir John James, who in turn entrusted her to the care of the Honorary Secretary of Penlee, Andrew Munson.

The second was the more elaborate naming ceremony of the *Ivan Ellen* in front of over four hundred invited guests. There was a special poignancy in the proceedings, since the legacy which enabled her purchase came from the father of lifetime RNLI servant John Leech, who had been stationed as relief mechanic at Penlee while the new crew were being trained after the loss of the *Solomon Browne*. She was named after his parents, and John himself made the presentation.

The third was a quieter event, to commemorate the gift of Mr Harold Lane Cox, a retired engineer who had lived near Truro. The Severn Class needs regular access and a proper mooring with electrical and water services. Thus Mr Cox's legacy was dedicated to the provision of a pontoon and ramp. This had the added bonus of making the lifeboat accessible to visitors, especially after the dictates of Health and Safety had decreed that it was too hazardous for the public to make the 50m trip in an open punt, even with several experienced life-savers at hand.

Penlee was thus transformed into one of the best-equipped stations in the country, a magnificent vote of confidence in its illustrious past and its crucial role in the future.

Penlee, like all other lifeboat stations, does not just consume funds but works very hard to provide them. The work of the Ladies Guild (a title now being phased-out) and other supporters is less dangerous and less glamorous than that of the crew, but it is the seed-corn of the RNLI. Throughout the year, on duty in the souvenir shop, on stalls, on windy corners with collecting-boxes, selling tickets, counting up change, organising fund-raising events and in other ingenious ways, the Guild has amassed a total contribution to be proud of, currently little short of £50,000 annually towards the RNLI's central funds. The RNLI needs nearly £60 million per annum, and it is an essential part of its traditions that none of this comes from government sources. It exists only because so many people want it to, and back their ideals with hard work and hard cash.

The work of the shore-based officers, subjected to a complete re-organisation in 2004, is another invisible strand in the life of a station. The Honorary Secretary (now Lifeboat Operations Manager) is in charge of all operational decisions ashore. He is supported by Deputy Launching Authorities and regular shore helpers. An Honorary Medical Officer and Deputy are always available if required. The branch has until recently been run by a President, a Chairman, their Deputies, a Press Officer and a committee, all of whom did much to keep the station going in the dark days of December 1981. The tradition of service is perhaps best exemplified in recent times by D L (Del) Johnson, who served the station for over 45 years, many of them as Honorary Secretary, was awarded the RNLI Silver Badge, Gold Badge and Bar, and had been granted the highest accolade of Honorary Life Governor shortly before his untimely death in 2001.

Del Johnson.
(Rosalie Johnson
collection).

After 200 years, the station finds itself in good shape. It has not only the best of operational equipment but an equally able team of people to run it. The Coxswain, Neil Brockman, became a lifeboat volunteer in his teens and was appointed coxswain at the young age of 28. He carries on the traditions of the RNLI in general and Penlee in particular, and also a family legacy, as his father perished with the *Solomon Browne* on a night when he himself was spared by Trevelyan Richards' decision to take only one from any family.

A deputy second coxswain/mechanic is also employed by the RNLI, Patrick "Patch" Harvey, another highly experienced crew-member and fisherman, who knows from personal experience (see records of 17/12/1999) how welcome the sight of a lifeboat can be.

Other officers include two second coxswains, a mechanic and two assistant mechanics, six experienced helmsmen for the Atlantic 75, plus a mechanic and a tractor driver/mechanic, together with a pool of enrolled crew numbering over twenty.

It's not all hard work...Penlee servants past and present. (Neil Brockman collection).

Between shouts there is a continuing workload. The Severn class needs daily attention, and has a planned schedule of maintenance to be followed. Crew training is also an ongoing commitment, involving weekly meetings, and a programme of 'competence-based' training in which all crew are trained in every discipline required - navigation, handling, radio, first aid, mechanics etc. The provisions of the magnificent new Lifeboat College at Poole also now include a mandatory course in sea survival for all crews. New crews have to be assessed and inducted into the training programme. The existing officers are also required to attend many other courses. There are regular inspections from Headquarters, and, of course, there is an ever-increasing load of paperwork.

The boat has a routine run-out every fortnight, and takes part in regular exercises with RNAS and RAF helicopters, with whom co-operation is so often an essential feature of a real-life rescue. There are also larger-scale exercises with other lifeboats and services, and regular liaison with the police, fire crews, coastguards and the National Coastwatch Institution. The lifeboats turn out for public demonstrations on fund-raising days, the Newlyn Fish Festival and the Annual Lifeboat Open-air Service, amongst other voluntary calls.

When the bleepers go off, Penlee is fortunate in its situation in a busy harbour where many crew-members are readily at hand; but even in the dead of night there will usually be less than ten minutes between receiving the first call and slipping the moorings.

Above all a first-class lifeboat is ready to go and a well-trained crew is ready to cope with distress and danger, all day and night, all week, all year, every year. Most of the members of the complex organisation who ensure this are volunteers, giving up their time to do what they do - from selling raffle tickets to manning the boat - for the same basic reason; that when the call comes, someone will be there to answer. They walk in the footsteps of a fine tradition. The story of Penlee goes on.

THE END

Emergency relief lifeboat arrives :
70' Clyde *Charles Henry Barrett (Civil Service No 35)* staffed by 4 RNLI Staff Crew and local crew - new volunteers start training at once.

Relief Watson *Charles Henry Ashley* takes over.

6/1/82	:	Answered a distress signal - false alarm.
5/2/82	:	Third relief lifeboat, Watson *Guy & Clare Hunter* (Isles Of Scilly Lifeboat 1955-1981) arrives, with Staff Coxswain Tam Beattie and Staff Mechanic John Leech.
8/4/82	:	Shout to FV *Halcyon*, saving vessel and two crew.
1/5/82	:	Overdue rowing boat - search carried out without result.
7/8/82	:	Flares - search found nothing.
29/8/82	:	Flares - search found nothing.
30/8/82	:	Yacht meeting adverse conditions - others coped.
16/9/82	:	Punt overdue - found and towed in with two crew.
19/9/82	:	Distress alert - probable hoax.
18/12/82	:	Distress alert - false alarm.

1983

2/4/83	:	Ferry *Armorique* came into bay with fire on board, not in danger - passengers evacuated - Penlee took off 38.
2/4/83	:	On way back rescued two wind-surfers in difficulties - out from 11.45 - 19.35.
22/4/83	:	Called to drifting MV *Wilgo* drifting onto a lee shore in force 9 winds off Porthleven having lost anchor and partial power, escorted until she reached Penzance.
Sunday 8th May	:	Arun Class *Mabel Alice,* identification number 52-24, (ON 1085) placed in service at 0001.
10/05/83	:	French trawler *Rayon de Soleil* towed in, in mild weather, from Tater Dhu. Crew list : K Thomas; E Madron; M Inskip; RB Keates; P Wallis; F Wallis.
7/06/83	:	21' fishing boat *Julie Ann* overdue in dense fog - search undertaken. (She was eventually found close to Scilly six hours later).
16/07/83	:	Thick fog - *Mabel Alice* launched mid-morning to assist swimmers disorientated off Porthleven - returned to Newlyn to clean up lifeboat for naming ceremony - but tasked to go to Isles of Scilly to assist St Mary's lifeboat in searching for survivors from crash of British Airways helicopter - while returning, received call from Coastguard for "Penlee Lifeboat" but on responding *Mabel Alice* was told "No, the other Penlee Lifeboat". This turned out to be the relief Watson *Guy & Clare Hunter* which had been launched from Penlee boathouse in the interim to the aid of a small pleasure boat lost in the fog.

18/07/83 : *Mabel Alice* officially named by Duke of Kent.

Chairman of Penlee Dr Dennis Leslie retires - succeeded by Clive Bennetts.

19/07/83 : First call to a rubber dinghy blowing offshore at Praa Sands - rescued by others.

19/07/83 : Second call to assist after RNAS helicopter crashed into the sea in the same area - landed a body.

26/07/83 : Searched for missing speedboat off Porthleven - later found to be OK.

18/09/83 : Medico to large unidentified MV.

25/09/83 : Rough sea and fog - first call to fishing boat *Progress* having engine trouble and lost in fog - found, escorted and later towed into Newlyn.

25/09/83 : Second call - yacht *Jonadab* in trouble in rough seas - established tow with difficulty after 2 lifeboatmen transferred aboard - towed in with 4 crew - skipper and wife taken to hospital.

13/12/83 : Fishing boat *Lady Katherine* wrecked off Kemyel Point - gave assistance - two crew on rocks winched off by helicopter.

30/12/83 : Landed injured crewman from MFV *Frances Stevens*.

1984

5/02/84 : Landed injured crewman from large Danish cargo vessel *Kristine Sobye*.

20/02/84 : Landed injured crewman.

23/02/84 : Escorted dredger *Mersey 41* which was in difficulties in bad weather.

26/03/84 : Carried out search for missing diver off Lamorna, with no result.

2/06/84 : Unidentified trimaran capsized 8 miles SE of Tater Dhu in very rough force 7-9 conditions - one crew saved and yacht safely towed in, upside-down.

3/09/84 : First call to the yacht *Alto* with three crew at risk of driving onto shore at Rinsey Head - towed in.

3/09/84 : Unidentified yacht towed in from behind Penzance harbour wall in bad conditions, earning Letter of Thanks from the Director of the RNLI.

9/09/84 : Medico to large MV *Fanafrost*.

13/11/84 : Two launches to false alarms.

1985

15/02/85 : The French trawler *St Simeon* sprang a leak and lost power in easterly force 10-11, later described as "violent and freezing conditions" and "the worst channel storm for years" - Penlee took over tow off Lizard from Falmouth LB which had been towing her upwind for 12 hours - too dangerous to run for Mounts Bay or Falmouth, so made for Plymouth - towed for 9 hours during height of storm, then passed tow to Plymouth LB. Unfortunately *St Simeon* sank while nearing Plymouth.

31/03/85 : Motor yacht *Njord* escorted to Newlyn in SSW gale.

2/04/85 : Two bathers reported in difficulties off Loe Bar - recalled when safely ashore.

6/04/85 : Rubber dinghy with engine failure off Lamorna - towed in

27/04/85 : Local fishing boat *Silver Spray* reported overdue, but later reached port unassisted.

6/05/85 : Four boys swept off Lands End - *Mabel Alice* joined search from 17.05 to nightfall, without result.

12/05/85 : Called to yacht *Tally Ho* - took over tow from assisting vessel, but yacht suddenly sank on way in - saved crew of one, plus a dog.

2/06/85 : Escorted in yacht *Mary* with broken mast.

12/06/85 : Two crew on yacht *Sirius Sarmauria* reported injured in westerly gale south of the Lizard - transferred doctor (Dr Hersant) to the yacht, but casualties too ill to transfer back, so escorted to Falmouth - 18 hour service 03.00 - 21.00.

20/08/85 : Escorted cabin cruiser with engine trouble to St Michaels Mount.

One man and his dog rescued from yacht *Tally Ho*, May 1985 – l to r Phil Wallis, Bobby Keates, *Tally Ho* owner, Roy Pascoe, Mike Hersant, Andrew Munson, Neil Brockman. (Andrew Besley).

12/09/85 : Searched for bather off Praa Sands - later found to be OK.

20/10/85 : Yacht *Tala-Hina* reported to be in trouble - eventually found nine miles from reported position - towed in together with crew of two adults and a boy.

24/10/85 : Called to assist search for man overboard from FV *Bonny Mary* - searched for 5 hours but no-one found.

28/10/85 : FV *Diane Marie* from Mullion reported engine failure 14 miles S of Newlyn - taken in tow and on arrival crew of 1 handed over to police - suspected of having stolen the boat.

1986

27/01/86 : Call to yacht *Double Cross* reported to be sinking in severe weather 28 miles south of the station - assisted to pump and escorted vessel safely to Newlyn.

14/02/86 : Coaster *Roy Clemo* lost an anchor while trying to shelter from SE gale - escorted to Penzance.

11/03/86 : Medico to Russian factory ship *Diplot*, landed one injured man and two helpers.

30/03/86 : Person reported in the water off the promenade at 00.23 - managed to reach shore unaided.

12/06/86 : Launch to tow in small fishing vessel, recalled when others coped.

24/06/86 : French yacht *Naviloc* taken in tow with broken rudder, brought into Newlyn.

25/08/86 : In southerly gale and very rough sea, called to yacht *Nasty* 25 miles to SE - too rough to pass a tow or even to close in and take off crew of two, who were brought across on lines – yacht sank a few minutes later.

29/08/86 : Round-the -world rower Geoff Cooper came to grief in choppy seas - helicopter rescued rower, while Penlee took the rowing-boat *Water Rat* into Newlyn.

8/11/86 : Towed in MFV *Carrie Ann* after engine breakdown.

1987

(Relief Arun *Duchess of Kent*)

18/01/87 : Towed in MFV *Michael & David* after engine trouble in strong SE wind.

3/02/87 : Medico to freighter *Lerma*.

2/04/87 : Called to assist after car went over the end of pier at Porthleven - carried out long search in 'Y' boat - 'Y'-boat capsized forcing Robert Marks and Joey Jeffery to scramble ashore, before refloating - search eventually prevented by low tide – no-one found.

22/04/87 : MFV *Enterprise* fouled prop with chain off Lamorna - problem solved "...with junior hacksaw" and vessel escorted into Newlyn.

Survivors from yacht *Nasty*, – lucky to be alive (Phil Monkton)

10/05/87 : MFV *Pioneer* went ashore on rocks near Tater Dhu - pumped and escorted to safety.

(*Mabel Alice*)

1/07/87 : Trawler *Kaylee* from Brixham developed gearbox trouble, requiring a long tow into Newlyn from 16.40 - 23.45.

9/08/87 : Medico to sick person in yacht *Tjeldoy* off Penzance harbour during helicopter demonstration off promenade.

10/08/87 : Medico to Dutch FV *Hilde Jacoba*.

30/08/87 : Left annual lifeboat service in Mousehole to carry out medico to bulk carrier *Durrington*.

31/08/87 : In SE wind, rough sea and heavy swell, called to broken down inflatable with six divers aboard - when reached only 20' from rocks - towed into deeper water where all six safely transferred, and taken with their boat to Newlyn. Six saved, under Coxswain Edwin Madron.

27/09/87 : Fishing boat *Patricia Morwenna* with engine trouble towed into Porthleven.

4/10/87 : Yacht *Solitaire* taken under tow off Carn Dhu in easterly gale, towed into Newlyn.

16/10/87 : Assisted when helicopter ditched to west of Porthleven - second helicopter rescued crew - lifeboat attempted to secure helicopter which was driving ashore. While doing so experienced sudden 60' freak wave close to shore - Edwin Madron called to crew to hold on and throttled up to breast the wave, burying lifeboat up to her superstructure on other side "...like hitting concrete". The incident was caught on video.

30/10/87 : RNLI lifeboat ON 1029 on passage from Troon suffered engine failure off Runnelstone - towed into Newlyn.

31/12/87 : Child washed off Loe Bar - searched with lifeboat and 'Y' boat, in vain.

1988

10/02/88 : Belgian trawler *Normauwil* stranded on Cressar rocks, Eastern Green - towed clear with much difficulty due to jammed rudder, and taken to Newlyn. (c/f service to same vessel in similar position off Newlyn north pier by *Solomon Browne* in March 1980).

28/02/88 : Call to capsized rubber dinghy, no service required.

28/03/88 : Falmouth fishing vessel 'FH 441' towed in after experiencing steering failure off Praa Sands.

29/04/88 : Search for man fallen off cliff near Cudden Point - nothing found.

26/06/88 : On routine engine run, two boys on dinghy found unable to start outboard motor - towed in. (ON 963).

20/07/88 : After collision between FV *Lilian J* and French FV *Steren an Esperance*, latter found to be taking in water - long service (nearly 8 hours) as she had to be towed stern-first.

28/08/88 : During demonstration for Gala Day, *Mabel Alice* called to overturned speedboat *Thin Blue Liner* near Lamorna - crew rescued by helicopter - speedboat righted and towed to Newlyn.

3/09/88 : Took over tow of yacht *Halcyon* with engine trouble off Marazion and towed in.

18/09/88 : FV *New Pioneer* wrecked off Merthen Point near St Loy - three crew took to liferaft and found clinging to rocks - taken off with difficulty and brought safely home.

25/09/88 : Red flares - false alarm.

Peter Garnier appointed Chairman.

22/12/88 : French FV *Elfin Des Mers* called for assistance with fouled propeller 23 miles to S - towed in.

1989

3/01/89 : Inflatable from warship *Orkney* overturned in rough seas - survivors found washed up on beach - all OK.

4/02/89 : Call to FV *Trident* with fouled propeller on a rough and cold morning - towed into Newlyn.

20/03/89 : Escorted leaking FV *Stillwater Again* to Newlyn.

10/04/89 : Medico to FV *Brittania IV*.

11/07/89 : Exercise with District Inspector disrupted when services required to a swamped dinghy off Praa Sands - dealt with before arrival...

11/07/89 : ...and again when called to small boat stranded on St Clements Island - again resolved by the time the lifeboat arrived. Exercise then presumably completed.

5/08/89 : Boy reported missing off Wherrytown beach, having been swimming in rubber ring - searched with 'Y'-boat - boy found on beach and taken to hospital by helicopter.

14/09/89 : Call to coaster *Tresco*, in trouble with a cargo shift - recalled when taken in tow by others.

(*AJR & LG Uridge*) to end of year

19/09 89 : Long night-time tow of French FV *Tor-Pen* from 7 miles SSE of the Wolf Rock in worsening conditions - 22.35 - 04.00.

20/09/89 : With little time to rest, called to German yacht *Velra* ashore off Penzance - passed line with 'Y'-boat and kept gentle strain on to avoid further stranding for two hours until tide flooded her clear, then towed to Newlyn - "...not even a thank-you".

1/10/89 : Motor yacht *Sea Ranger* with engine trouble 3 miles W of Longships - towed in.

Newlyn Harbourmaster Andrew Munson appointed as Honorary Secretary.

24/11/89 : Padstow trawler *Flamingo* capsized 5 miles to SW of station - long search for missing crew, but none found.

29/11/89 : Ketch *Shoran* disabled with engine failure and ripped sails 7 miles to SW in force 8 gale - safely towed in.

The Y-boat carries a line to the yacht *Velra* off Eastern Green, September 1989. (Neil Brockman collection).

(*Mabel Alice*)

24/01/90 : Medico to Russian ship *Kara.*

22/03/90 : Man reported in the water off Penzance promenade - rescued after short search and passed to the helicopter for transport to hospital.

9/04/90 : Confusion as boy reported fallen overboard from speed-boat - original casualty found to have swum to tug to raise alarm - second boy found to be still in boat - towed in.

26/04/90 : Large cabin cruiser *Princess Angelina* - lost in poor visibility - found and escorted.

24/05/90 : On exercise in the bay spotted a windsurfer in difficulties due to exhaustion - towed to Marazion beach.

26/05/90 : Yacht *Nirvana* reported engine failure 7 miles to W in an E gale - escorted while coming in under sail.

22/06/90 : FV *Small* reported to be overdue - later found to be safe.

22/07/90 : After a demonstration off the promenade, called to cabin cruiser *L.O.D.I.* drifting off Porthleven with engine failure - took off woman and four small children and towed into Porthleven.

26/07/90 : French yacht *Adagio* aground behind Albert Pier - towed clear as tide rose.

22/07/90 : Body reported in water off Penzance - found and recovered.

29/07/90 : Flares sighted off Penzance - crew, on way to celebration lunch, turned out to search - believed to be deliberate false alarm - crew took late lunch.

19/08/90 : Small local sailing dinghy reported overdue in poor visibility - found to be under tow.

24/08/90 : Yacht *Beggars Banquet* grounded behind Albert Pier in fog - took off three crew - later safely towed off.

15/09/90 : FV *Le Petite Anglaise* fouled propeller off Penzance in rough seas and strong southerly wind - towed into Penzance.

22/10/90 : Body reported in sea off Lamorna - found and recovered.

25/10/90 : 04.00 shout to yacht *Vieux Garcon III* having difficulties in adverse conditions - towed in.

15/11/90 : Person reported missing after cliff fall near Loe bar - no-one found.

27/11/90 : FV *Hollie Jane* from Grimsby towed in after engine failure.

25/12/90 : Body reported in water off Penzance promenade in strong westerly winds - nothing found.

13/01/91 : No lifeboat involved, but Deputy Coxswain Edwin Madron, and crewmembers Neil Brockman and Rob Cooke succeeded after a long struggle in turning around a Fin Whale which had become trapped on rocks near Mousehole - whale swam off to deeper waters.

12/02/91 : Red flares reported off St Michael's Mount - nothing found.

16/02/91 : Went to assistance of MV *Rocqvaine* from Nassau - being towed in with engine trouble by the *Gry Maritha* - helped three times to refix tow and escorted in.

8/03/91 : Medico at 0400 to Cypriot MV *Nortrader*.

(Relief Arun *Margaret Russel Fraser*)

21/04/91 : Towed in fishing boat *Golden Dolphin*.

(*Mabel Alice*)

9/06/91 : Medico to US submarine tender *Simon Lake* - took off two crewmen in rough conditions.

18/06/91 : Another medico to the above - took off a woman crewmember.

Jim Hodge, Honorary Treasurer since 1962 and holder of RNLI Gold Badge, elected President.

30/06/91 : Tug *Sea Viper* reported aground on Runnlestone - crew taken off by passage lifeboat en route to Isle of Man - *Mabel Alice* made repeated attempts to tow vessel off - succeeded in doing so, but *Sea Viper* sank soon afterwards under tow by tug *Goliath*.

26/07/91 : Local FV *Confide* reported taking water 12 miles to SW - transferred two crew and an extra pump and escorted home.

28/07/91 : Small FV *Palores* with four crew spotted with fouled propeller off Penlee, about to go onto rocks - towed in.

7/08/91 : Small punt reported overdue off Praa Sands with five boys aboard - found to be OK shortly after launch.

21/08/91 : Medico to yacht *Trienda* while on exercise with Divisional Inspector - gave assistance to crewmember and escorted to Newlyn.

28/08/91 : Bather reported missing off Praa Sands - found to have swum ashore.

18/11/91 : Red flares off Perranuthnoe proved to be small St Ives FV *Dino* - adrift in WNW gale - rescued two crew and towed in.

20/11/91 : Medico to Dutch FV *Cornelis Vrolijk FZN* - landed a sick man.

24/11/91 : Medico to FV *Morning Sun*, under tow by Newlyn FV *Filadelfia* after fire onboard - landed three crew in Newlyn.

24/11/91 : Recalled to *Morning Sun* - now taking water in very heavy seas - transferred pump and two crew with great difficulty - pumped and escorted into Newlyn - total service 10.05 - 17.00
Commendation received for Kenny Thomas.

24/12/91 : Took out an engineer to *Gry Maritha* to sort out engine failure.

(Relief Arun *ARJ & LG Uridge*)

12/02/92 : Medico to tug *Boa Pride* to take off an injured man.

16/02/92 : Newlyn FV *Marianne* towed in with engine failure.

(*Mabel Alice*)

12/04/92 : Yacht *Biskit* in trouble with broken mast and sails in the water - sails reset and escorted.

5/06/92 : FV *Jean Pierre Andre* - took over tow from Lizard LB, brought into Newlyn.

7/06/92 : Early morning shout at 03.45 to *Confide* - towed in with engine failure.

16/06/92 : Dutch yacht *Chinook* found to be drifting quietly out of the bay, with three crew asleep below - crew awoken...

21/06/92 : Reports of three people stranded on rocks between Logan Rock and Pedn Vounder - no-one found.

23/06/92 : Medico to French FV *Mousse*.

23/07/92 : Long night's service - 22.53 - 05.30 - to tow in FV *Steren An Mor* from breakdown 32 miles to SSW.

30/07/92 : Another night tow to FV *Fleur de Lys* - adrift with fouled propeller.

Seeing double – *Mabel Alice* on right and on the left, frequent relief lifeboat *A J R & L G Uridge*. (Phil Monkton).

4/10/92 : 'Mirror' sailing dinghy seen to be capsized off Mousehole - righted and escorted into Mousehole.

Kenny Thomas moves to France - Neil Brockman appointed Coxswain at 28 - Mike Atkinson as second Cox.

28/11/92 : Three surfers reported in difficulties off Praa Sands - helicopter called - found to be OK.

1993

4/04/93 : Yacht *Skeaby Ny Tonn* struck rocks off St Clements Island in the dark and a force 9 SW gale - recovered by *Mabel Alice* a mile to the east and safely towed in.

16/05.93 : Call to yacht *Sharvelle* reported overdue - found to be OK.

28/05/93 : FV *Silver Spray* reported engine failure 10 miles to S - towed in.

21/06/93 : Yacht *Kamakura* aground in Lamorna - floated off as LB arived.

21/06/93 : On way back from above gave first aid to crewman aboard FV *W S Stevenson*.

1/07/93 : Yacht *Jon M* taken in tow from 6 miles S of station.

11/07/93 : Missing person reported off Praa Sands - no-one found.

18/07/93 : While on exercise windsurfer spotted in difficulties with broken sail - sail fixed by crew member - windsurfer returned to beach.

10/08/93 : Assembly at 23.30 after reports of man overboard from FV *Kingfisher* - man swam into Newlyn and presented himself in the assembly building as crew on punt preparing to launch...

15/08/93 : 05.00 called to FV *Heather Lea II* taking in water 6 miles to S - pumped and escorted in at 06.45.

15/08/93 : 21.15 called to Yarmouth FV *Alida T*, with fire in engine room - started tow, but fire flared up so four crew taken off - fire kept under control - towed into Newlyn at 00.45.

20/08/93 : Towed in FV *Harvester* of St Ives - fouled propeller.

22/08/93 : Medico to large Dutch trawler *Franziska*.

22/08/93 : Small speedboat drifting ashore at Roskilly in rough sea with two aboard - crewman swam to speedboat with line and towed to safety.

23/08/93 : Medico to German yacht *Gollum*.

19/09/93 : Medico to Dutch trawler *Dirk Diezerk*.

19/09/93 : Small dinghy *Solitaire* with three youngsters aboard escorted from Penzer Point in poor weather.

25/09/93 : Yacht *Sea Tangle* unable to make headway off Praa Sands - towed in.

9/10/93 : Small FV reported overdue - false alarm.

31/10/93 : Medico to Italian cargo vessel *Aquarius*.

(ARJ & LG Uridge)

14/12/93 : Large Ukranian cargo vessel *Kapitan Dzuashevich* escorted into Mounts Bay with 25 degree list due to cargo shift.

Escorting the listing Ukranian cargo vessel *Kapitan Dzuashevich* into Mounts Bay. (Tim Stevens).

1994

3/01/94 : Medico to large Spanish FV.

12/01/94 : Inflatable servicing Ukranian cargo vessel escorted to safety after springing a leak.

13/01/94 : Inflatable servicing Ukranian cargo vessel taken in tow after breakdown.

17/01/94 : Missing diver failed to surface off Lamorna Cove - no-one found.

(Mabel Alice)

13/02/94 : Escorted trawler *Elizabeth Ann* under tow in gale force conditions and helped into Newlyn.

21/02/94 : Towed in FV *Bonny Mary* from Tater Dhu, adrift with rudder damage.

27/02/94 : Man and boy washed off quay at Porthleven - unable to reach man in surf boy winched up by helicopter but also died two days later.

30/03/94 : Medico in bad weather to coaster *Natasha C.*

25/04/94 : Medico to Newlyn FV *Twilight III* in poor conditions - HMA Peter Cox and Roy Pascoe forced to jump onto casualty.
Letters of Thanks to both from RNLI Chief of Operations.

29/04/94 : Small inflatable broken down off Tater Dhu - escorted into Lamorna.

(Relief Arun *Duke of Atholl*)

7/06/94 : Small punt reported missing from Newlyn - owner's bike still on quay - LB searched as far as Penberth - owner found to be asleep in St Just - bike had broken down - whereabouts of punt unknown.

25/06/94 : Small aircraft crashed in sea by Greeb Rocks off Perranuthnoe - two bodies recovered.

26/06/94 : After demonstration off Penzance promenade, called to red flares off Cudden Point - small fishing boat broken down, towed into St Michael's Mount.

26/06/94 : Searched for missing walker near Lamorna - later found OK.

3/07/94 : Red flares off Mousehole - fishing boat towed into Mousehole by others.

(*Mabel Alice*)

18/07/94 : Launched to assist small FV but recalled.

31/07/94 : Launched to assist small FV but recalled.

8/08/94 : Yacht *Lady Glow* in difficulties off Gwennap Head in strong SE winds - towed in.

8/08/94 : Yacht *Surf Dancer* in difficulties in same position - towed in.

26/08/94 : Catamaran *Shere Khan* towed in from St Michael's Mount after breakdown.

17/09/94 : Day-long service to ex RN WWII launch *Calshot* adrift with engine failure 10 miles west of Wolf Rock - towed in after seven hours.

6/11/94 : Search for missing walker off Lamorna - no-one found.

2/12/94 : Assisted when man fell in sea off Porthleven - body recovered by helicopter.

6/12/94 : Night call to Newlyn crabber *Julian Paul* with fouled propeller in severe conditions 4 miles west of Longships - initially taken in tow by Sennen LB but unable to make headway in gale force south-westerlies.
Mabel Alice attempted tandem tow with Sennen, but Sennen's tow would not hold in conditions so Penlee towed alone with *Four Boys* escorting - very slow headway in winds up to Force 12 - less than one knot to begin with - eventually increased to three knots - brought safely into Newlyn after eight hours.

BRONZE MEDAL SERVICE
Bronze Medal awarded to Coxswain Neil Brockman, presented by Duchess of Kent 18/05/95

Medal Certificates to Mike Atkinson, Joey Jeffery, Rob Cooke, Graham Henderson, Paul Ashworth and Graham Bray.

25/01/95 : Medico to Ukranian tug *Kondor* in Mounts Bay.

5/02/95 : Medico to Spanish FV Nuvodi Segumbo.

21/02/95 : Medico to Milford-registered trawler *Dwrgi.*

10/03/95 : Assisted FV *Ocean Spray* to tow and berth FV *Sardia Louise* in heavy weather.

13/03/95 : Stood by windsurfer west of St Michael's Mount - no assistance necessary.

9/04/95 : Yacht *Morwenna* called for assistance to crewmember suffering suspected heart attack - sadly died shortly after doctor arrived.

13/04/95 : Neil Brockman and Mike Atkinson spotted a small punt blowing ashore onto rocks near Mousehole - called for lifeboat while manhandling punt away from rocks to safety.

21/04/95 : FV *Mystique* - skipper Kenny Thomas - struck Outer Buck on way to fishing grounds, and sank in four minutes. *Mabel Alice* launched, but the crew of four were picked up by the FV *Brittania IV.*

21/04/95 : Yacht *Kostas* called in making no headway against NE wind and crew suffering from exhaustion - lifeboat crewman transferred and yacht safely towed to Newlyn.

27/04/95 : Small FV towed in from Lamorna after engine breakdown.

25/07/95 : Group of holidaymakers cut off by the tide at Bessy's Cove, near Prussia Cove - *Mabel Alice* stood by in choppy conditions, along with St Michael's Mount D-class, until group hauled to safety by cliff rescue team.

26/07/95 : FV *Ros Na Riogh* reported breakdown S of the Runnelstone - towed in.

13/09/95 : Search for small boat reported in trouble off Greeb Rock - nothing found.

20/09/95 : Small inflatable with three occupants seen in difficulties off Perranuthnoe - towed in.

5/10/95 : Medico to Dutch trawler *Zeeland.*

6/10/95 : Trawler *Ygraine* reported loss of steering 35 miles SSE of Newlyn - *Mabel Alice* launched at 0200 in heavy seas and force 7-9 SW winds - took up tow, which parted twice - succeeded in towing into Newlyn after 10 hour service.

15/10/95 : Medico to Dutch trawler *Cornelis Vrolijk.*

16/10/95 : Took engineer to container ship *Super Seven.*

20/10/95 : Towed in broken down FV *Jackie G* in quiet conditions.

26/10/95 : Another medico to *Cornelis Vrolijk.*

10/12/95 : Dutch trawler *Bayona* reported breakdown due to overheating - towed in.

25/12/95 : 19.05 on Christmas evening, called to catamaran *Laura of Colne* - engine broken down and mainsail blown out - towed her back to Newlyn, singing carols all the way home.

31/12/95 : 0400 on New Year's Eve, called to FV *Tudor Owen*, suffering from fouled propeller.

17/01/96 : Called to yacht *Shakatak*, broken down off Tater Dhu - towed to Newlyn.

20/01/96 : Another engine breakdown by catamaran *Laura of Colne*, off Penzance - towed in.

20/01/96 : Call to *Julian Paul*, again with fouled propeller, but this time only a mile off Lamorna - towed in.

29/02/96 : Medico to passenger boat *St Helena* to land a female casualty.

20/04/96 : Called to investigate abandoned yacht *Rumbumble* found drifting 10 miles S of The Lizard - some evidence of a fire but no clues as to whereabouts of crew - searched area in vain and towed yacht in.

8/05/96 : Stood by a canoeist in choppy conditions, escorted to safety.

7/06/96 : Yacht *Avocette III* towed in after fouling propeller.

11/06/96 : Russian sailing yacht *St Nicholas* started dragging anchor towards Eastern Green beach, but under way by the time *Mabel Alice* arrived - escorted to Newlyn.

20/06/96 : Medico to passenger liner *Regina Renaissance*.

13/07/96 : Took over tow of large FV *Intuition* 18 miles S of Newlyn - brought into Newlyn four hours later.

8/08/96 : Took over tow of yacht *Chinaman* in rough conditions, from passage Severn class 17-02- towed in.

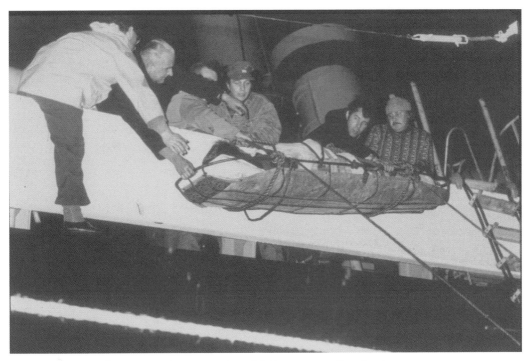

Night Medico - lowering the casualty. (M Hersant collection).

25/08/96 : Night tow of small FV *Jackie G* - hard to find as lights had failed, but found under flares and towed in.

4/09/96 : Night search for missing boy off Porthleven - proved to be hoax.

20/11/96 : French trawler *Buggin* coming in with partial engine failure - escorted through gaps.

22/11/96 : Escorted ex RN motor launch *Fantasia* to harbour in heavy weather.

25/11/96 : Medico to tug *Anglian Earl*.

1997

(*Mabel Alice*)

19/02/97 : Call at 23.30 in a WNW force 9 and heavy seas to Irish coaster *Innesfree* - drifting ashore two miles W of Longships with complete loss of power - on way report that anchors had checked her drift, allowing LB to reduce speed in head seas - shortly after arrival on scene, together with Sennen LB, *Innesfree's* engines re-started - both lifeboats returned to Newlyn.

28/02/97 : Search for man overboard from French FV *Martolod Breizh* near Wolf Rock - no-one found.

5/05/97 : Small MV *Boy One* reported engine trouble close to the Runnelstone - *Mabel Alice* stood by and escorted safely to anchorage in Mounts Bay.

13/05/97 : Call to person cut off by the tide - called off when found to be safe.

28/05/97 : Escorted local FV who was worried about shortage of fuel...

20/06/97 : Dinghy taken from Penzance harbour at about 3 am by three drunken youths - *Mabel Alice* found them rowing out to sea - brought back to Penzance, handed over to police.

2/07/97 : Catamaran *Ariel* called for assistance with engine failure off Tater Dhu - towed in.

23/07/97 : Local FV *Hayley H* suffered engine fire 8 miles S of station - extinguished fire, but needed tow in - *Mabel Alice* obliged.

26/08/97 : Launch to assist French yacht *Virgule Follante* having difficulty making the gaps into Newlyn in S gale - escorted to safety.

28/08/97 : Urgent call to man washed into sea off Porthleven - recalled when man recovered by helicopter.

29/08/97 : Yacht *Valuna* seen dragging anchor behind Newlyn North Pier - tow passed with difficulty in shallows and yacht carefully taken to deeper water, and into harbour.

29/09/97 : FV *Three Brothers* being towed in by another FV started taking on water heavily 11miles S of Newlyn - *Mabel Alice* passed pump and two crew, who stabilised situation - escorted to Newlyn.

30/09/97 : *Hayley H* once more needed tow in after breakdown.

2/10/97 : *Petrel Dawn*, FV converted to cabin cruiser, called for assistance at 22.16 after loss of engine power, citing her position as "off Penzance harbour". After extensive fruitless search with LB and "Y" boat, asked casualty (who had no flares) to set light to something - still nothing seen. On returning to port, LB heard reports of casualty believed to be on fire off St Ives! It was the *Petrel Dawn* which had rounded Lands End without realising it. St Ives LB attended. *Mabel Alice's* service ended 00.28.

1998

5/02/98 : FV *Ben Ser Laxa* reported gear snagged on seabed 6 miles SE of Runnelstone - *Mabel Alice* gave assistance, but gear had to be abandoned - FV escorted in.

9/02/98 : Medico to French FV *Effera*.

3/04/98 : Windsurfer reported in trouble off Marazion - found to be OK.

20/04/98 : Small FV *Alizia Yasmine* fouled propeller near Runnelstone - towed in.

25/04/98 : Small dinghy *Minnow* seen making distress signals by Asst Mechanic Graham Henderson - found under tow by another small boat.

25/04/98 : Truro-registered FV *Intuition* reported drifting ashore without power near Lamorna - tow established and FV brought in with 6 crew.

10/05/98 : Diving vessel sinking off Lamorna - occupants rescued by second diving vessel - swamped boat recovered and beached in Lamorna Cove.

17/05/98 : Short service to St Clements Island where three boys stranded - taken off by others before LB arrived.

24/05/98 : Diver surfaced with suspected 'bends' off Low Lee buoy - stood by while casualty winched into helicopter.

27/05/98 : Night service 22.10 - 04.00 to take over tow of 82' 1912 steam drifter *Feasible* from St Ives LB - broken down in attempt to steam from Penzance to Bristol - slow progress on account of her weight and long wait to enter harbour on account of her deep draught - *Mabel Alice* herself suffered engine trouble during tow.

(Relief Arun *Edith Emilie*)

6/06/98 : Small Falmouth FV *Sovereign* broken down in Mounts Bay - towed in.

8/07/98 : Escorted while dismasted yacht *Jeremy* towed in by French FV.

8/07/98 : Second call to *Feasible*, again broken down, this time off Tater Dhu.

(*Mabel Alice*)

21/07/98 : Crewman taken ill on catamaran *Pendragon* 6 miles S - helicopter took off casualty - Penlee crew sailed yacht into Newlyn, with *Mabel Alice* in attendance.

9/08/98 : Local FV *Four Sisters* broke down off Wolf Rock - towed in.

2/09/98   :   Early call 05.47 for third service to *Feasible* - again broken down off Tater Dhu - towed in as usual.

Peter Garnier retires as Chairman - replaced by former Penlee Honorary Medical Adviser Dr Mike Hersant.

25/10/98 :   Call to St Clements Island to children stranded - FV took children off, *Mabel Alice* recovered dinghy and returned it to Mousehole.

11/12/98 :   Medico to large Dutch trawler *Frank Bonnefass* - crewman taken off in difficult conditions.

18/12/98 :   Second medico to *Frank Bonefass* - though different casualty - crewman again taken off in difficult conditions.

1999

21/03/99 :   Medico to merchantman *Lady Serena*.

27/03/99 :   Confused call after a 'Pan' alert to a dismasted yacht seen off Gwennap Head - which was in no difficulty, but on passage to Plymouth for a new mast.

2/04/99   :   Took over tow of yacht *Skyla B* from Sennen LB - towed in.

16/04/99 :   Service to small FV *Hawkwind* 2 miles off Tater Dhu with disabled steering gear - towed in.

23/04 99 :   FV *Jessica Poppy* towed in after fouling propeller near Tater Dhu.

(Relief Arun *Elizabeth Ann*)

16/05/99 :   Diver with suspected bends recovered and given oxygen - taken to ambulance.

4/06/99   :   Call at 02.15 to search for man missing in vicinity of Penzance wet dock - unable to enter wet dock because of tide - decided on shore search, so re-moored LB in Newlyn and returned by road - 'casualty' found asleep locked in public toilets on quay - service ended 04.00.

6/07/99   :   Small FV *Danda* with gearbox failure off Loe Bar - towed into Porthleven.

6/08/99   :   Yacht *Pippin II* called for assistance at 02.04, unsure of her position in a rising SE wind - believed herself to be S of Newlyn but eventually found 9 miles to SE - escorted to Newlyn.

7/08/99   :   Second night call in succession, to trawler *Harm Johannes*, with fouled propeller in Force 5 ESE wind - towed in.

24/08/99 :   Yacht *Island Mac* seen drifting without power off Low Lee by Penlee Hon Sec (who was on the *Scillonian*) - towed in to Newlyn.

11/09/99 :   Call to Penzance harbour - man fallen off inflatable dinghy in harbour - casualty recovered by others, but inflatable still speeding around harbour in tight circle, unmanned - LB crew formed a lassoo from heaving line and succeeded in fouling inflatable's propeller - recovered dinghy and checked casualty.

1/10/99   :   Launched in response to emergency distress signal coming from direction of Penzance harbour - after search, signal confirmed to be false alarm.

(*Mabel Alice*)

16/10/99 : FV *Conquest* broken down 3 miles off Newlyn - towed in.

26/10/99 : Long search for fisherman swept off rocks at Rinsey - no-one found.

27/10/99 : Resumed search for missing fisherman - helicopter recovered a body.

10/11/99 : Medico at 04.22 to passenger ferry *Venus* - LB damaged by ferry's 18" 'belting' during transfer, but casualty safely brought ashore and transferred to ambulance.

10/12/99 : Medico to Antiguan coaster *Jackaranda*.

17/12/99 : Local FV *Penrose* began to sink after hauling in a huge catch of pilchards - only masthead light showing above water when *Mabel Alice* arrived on scene - three rescued, including Penlee crewmember Patrick "Patch" Harvey.

21/12/99 : Call to French trawler *Gwel A Vo* 35 miles S of Newlyn in heavy seas and 4-5 metre swells - trawler broken down and awaiting tow, but needing attention to seriously injured crewman - three crew transferred to trawler and succeeded in lowering casualty to LB deck in very difficult conditions, since the trawler drifting broadside without power - LB had to be turned smartly downwind to avoid casualty being washed off deck - recovered safely into wheelhouse, three crew recovered from trawler, and casualty taken to Newlyn after 7½ hour service.

Letter of Thanks from Chairman of RNLI to Neil Brockman, and Letters of Thanks to Patrick Harvey, David Osborne, David Pascoe and the rest of the crew.

2000

16/02/00 : Medico to FV *Conquest*.

11/03/00 : Another tow of the *Feasible* - broken down again off St Ives - tow transferred at Runnelstone.

Death of Peter Garnier

9/04/00 : Yacht *Fullmarks* seen to be making no progress off Runnelstone in NE Force 5/6 - towed in.

29/04/00 : Diving RIB reported drifting off Lamorna - towed in.

4/06/99 : FV *Anthony Stevenson* under tow by FV *Jacqueline* and taking in water - took over escort from Isles Of Scilly LB near Wolf Rock - passed pump, escorted safely to Newlyn.

26/06/00 : Medico to local fisherman Geoff Page - rescued after 5 hours with trapped hand - and assisted in recovery of his boat *Barbican Maid*.

30/06/00 : Call to assist 19-metre yacht *Jan Rorlan* being sailed by single crew, exhausted - towed in.

26/07/00 : Small FV *Danda* fouled propeller off Porthleven - once again towed into Porthleven.

All in a day's work – on the left one trawler is towing a broken down colleague, while another trawler takes a heavy sea on the right. *Mabel Alice,* almost invisible in a trough in the centre, stands by. (Neil Brockman collection).

31/07/00 : Pile of woman's clothes discovered at Penzance harbour at 22.53 - searched with lifeboat and "Y" boat - no-one found.

14/08/00 : Medico to tanker *Maersk Sussex.*

28/08/00 : Call to raft (from Newlyn raft race) taken out by two drunken men - men recovered and taken into Newlyn to police custody.

Binkie Wallen retires as Chair of Ladies Guild after 23 years - replaced by Janet Madron.

Death of John Corin, Penlee Public Relations Officer and lifeboat historian.

11/10/00 : Panamanian freighter *Star Anna* dragging anchor onto lee shore near St Michaels Mount - stood by and escorted to safety.

21/11/00 : Report of punt in difficulties - false alarm.

26/11/00 : Body in water off Battery Rocks - "Y" boat launched to assist recovery - body recovered by police from shore.

16/12/00 : Took over tow of small FV *Charlotte Louise* - towed in.

29/12/00 : Cable vessel *Dolfyn* wrecked just off Carn Topna, Mousehole - Neil Brockman inspected from shore before calling for launch at 23.44 - attended in rising swell and very shallow water - because of weather conditions and injured crewman took off 4 crew at once - unable to tow casualty off - brought crew into Newlyn

Letter of Commendation to Neil Brockman from Chief of Operations.

2001

4/01/01 : Medico to large cargo vessel *Rhine Carrier.*

20/01/01 : Stood by during rescue of two crew from capsized inflatable off Penzance harbour.

13/03/01 : Launch at 04.38 to large cargo vessel *Arklow Dawn* - drifting without power 6 miles S of Tater Dhu in W gale - recalled after casualty restarted engines.

Arrival of ILB Atlantic 75 *City of Bradford IV* in new boathouse - not forgetting Kevin the Tractor.

2/04/01 : Call to Newlyn FV *Edward Harvey* drifting with fouled propeller 9 miles to S of station - towed in.

4/05/01 : **ILB** Launch to children attempting to swim ashore after inflatable dinghy blown out to sea - called too late to render assistance.

10/05/01 : **ILB** Launched to assist small FV *Elle Mae* drifting 2 miles S of station - towed in.

17/05/01 : **ILB** Call to swimmer in difficulty off Penzance swimming pool - managed to reach shore unaided.

24/05/01 : **ILB** Disabled jet-ski at back of Penzance quay - towed into Newlyn.

10/06/01 : Called to E side of bay after an EPIRB distress signal received - found to be false alarm.

1/07/01 : Call from yacht *Iceberg* making little progress off Porthleven with single crew - towed to Newlyn.

27/07/01 : **ILB** Call to diving RIB - out of fuel - towed to beach at Marazion.

4/08/01 : **ILB** Sudden series of squalls during major dinghy race - called in to help St Michael's Mount "D" Class - tasked to assist capsized dinghies - diverted to reports of swimmer in trouble - swimmer reached shore - called across bay to group of dinghies near Tater Dhu - found to be coping - recalled to Marazion - helped two dinghies to beach - started tow of another dinghy with exhausted crew - called to windsurfer being washed against back of St Michael's Mount quay - passed tow of dinghy to rescue boat and recovered windsurfer - stood by until all other casualties out of danger.

5/08/01 : Medico to cargo vessel *Arklow Vale.*

5/09/01 : **ILB & ALB** As both LBs on evening exercise, both attended report of yacht aground on St Michael's Mount causeway - yacht *Sabravon* having cleared causeway escorted to Newlyn by ALB.

9/10/01 : Yacht *Bowman* called for assistance with steering failure - towed in.

14/10/01 : **ILB & ALB** Both LBs called when female walker suffered cliff fall east of Lamorna in thick fog - stood by while paramedics stabilised severely injured casualty - while preparing to take casualty off rocks, fog lifted sufficiently for helicopter to operate - casualty winched to safety.

Death of Del Johnson, former Honorary Secretary and Treasurer, holder of Gold Badge and Bar, after 45 years service to Penlee Station.

31/10/01 : Closure of St Michael's Mount "D" Class lifeboat station.

22/11/01 : **ILB** Call to dinghy reported adrift off Marazion - dinghy found to be empty and derelict - towed to Penzance.

19/12/01 : 20th Anniversary of loss of *Solomon Browne*.

25/12/01 : **ILB** Launch after report of red flares in the bay - found to have been let off ashore.

2002

10/01/02 : **ILB** Walker reported missing - found to be OK soon after launch.

21/01/02 : Called to escort French trawler *Ksora* - being towed in by another FV in SSW Force 7 - stood by until both vessels safe in harbour.

19/03/02 : **ILB** Call to reported 'person in water' off Penzance quay - after long search no-one found.

30/03/02 : **ILB** Call to swimmer in difficulties off Battery Rocks - man recovered from offshore rock with severe hypothermia - recovered after two days in intensive care.

8/04/02 : **ILB** called by Hon Sec to investigate unusual lights in bay - FV found to be OK.

21/04/02 : **ILB** Pleasure boat broken down off Penzance - towed into Penzance.

21/04/02 : FV *Lauren* broken down off Lamorna - towed in by *Mabel Alice*.

1/05/02 : **ILB & ALB** Body reported in sea off Loe Bar - after search in shallow water, body recovered from surf by Coastguards.

5/05/02 : Call to local FV *Sarah Steve* with broken fuel line off Lamorna - towed in.

(Relief Arun *City of Dublin/Mabel Alice*)

13/05/02 : ALB & ALB. Guernsey-registered FV *Chelaris J* reported having fouled own nets, drifting in heavy seas 25miles to S in SSE Force 8-9 gale. Relief Arun *City of Dublin* launched 06.20. On way in 6 metre waves, fell into deep trough and slammed, damaging fittings including "Y" boat - on scene fixed tow to casualty - tow parted, causing whiplash damage to aft of LB - tow re-established - on return *Mabel Alice*, back on station after repairs, launched with second crew to attach tow to rear to bring casualty through gaps in difficult conditions - casualty and both ALBs safely in harbour after 9¹/₂ hour service.

16/05/02 : **ILB** Towed broken-down pleasure boat *BJ* into Penzance.

30/05/02 : **ILB** Small FV *Alice Louise* from Porthleven fouled propeller in Mounts Bay - towed to Newlyn.

8/06/02 : Call to trawler *Stereden Va Bro* being towed in, on fire, by Sennen LB - stood by casualty while Sennen took crew to Newlyn - managed to extinguish fire with hoses - towed casualty to Newlyn where checked by Fire Brigade - 7 hour service.

19/09/02 : Another long service to racing yacht *Tom Crean* - dismasted after collision 50 miles SSW of station - three hour passage to casualty in poor visibility - brought into Newlyn after 9 hour service.

20/09/02 : **ILB** Launch to yacht *Gawot* - unsure of position.

21/09/02 : Stood by scalloper *Jacoba* - aground in Lamorna Cove - taken in tow by tug at high tide - escorted to Penzance - 11 hour service.

29/09/02 : 04.30 call to yacht *Zulu* reported missing by wife of owner - found by *Mabel Alice* after all-out search, anchored safely off Mullion - owner asleep - woken with foghorn.

9/10/02 : Call to trawler *William Sampson* adrift with engine trouble off Low Lee in Force 6 SE winds - towed in.

10/10/02 : Red flares reported in bay - nothing found.

11/12/02 : Red flares reported by passing tanker - searched from 03.07 - 05.46 - nothing found.

15/12/02 : Trawler *ABS* unable to recover fishing gear due to failed compressor - passed portable compressor - escorted casualty to Newlyn.

29/12/02 : Again to trawler *ABS* this time with engine trouble off Lamorna- escorted to Newlyn.

2003

26/01/03 : FV *Cathryn* taking water rapidly - passed salvage pump - escorted to Newlyn.

Mabel Alice taken out of service. Relief Arun on station.

12/03/03 Severn Class *Ivan Ellen* arrived on station.

Atlantic 75 *Paul Alexander* arrived on station

Bar to her Gold Badge awarded to Rosalie Johnson, and Gold Badge awarded to her mother Binkie Wallen

18/03/03 : **ILB & ALB** Red flares reported E of Praa Sands - both LBs searched but nothing found - first service for *Ivan Ellen*

21/03/03 : **ILB** Small pleasure boat broken down 3 miles S - towed in.

30/04/03 : Red flares reported off Mousehole - nothing found.

3/05/03 : Medico to large Spanish FV.

13/05/03 : **ILB** Small FV *Georgina B* towed in after breakdown off Low Lee.

20/06/03 : **ILB** Broken-down speedboat drifting off Praa Sands had been adrift in hot sun for three hours - female casualty treated for sun-stroke, and suddenly taken seriously ill before arrival in Porthleven - given oxygen - transferred to ambulance along with other crew.

24/06 03 : Brixham trawler *Semper Fidelis* out of fuel 12 miles S of station - towed in.

13/07/03 : All-night call to Finnish yacht *Lena* suffering from storm damage and engine breakdown - broken mast and sails tidied up and yacht towed in.

22/07/03 : Local small FV *Mizpah* caught fire near Newlyn - crew recovered from life-raft - fire extinguished by LB hoses -towed in to Newlyn.

29/07/03 : Local FV *Sovereign* fouled propeller off Lamorna - lines caught on bottom - freed and towed in.

29/07/03 : Yacht *Seaquester* reported lost rudder 16 miles S of station in Force 6-7 winds - towed in.

4/08/03 : **ILB** Yacht *Pilgrim of Tamar* began to drag anchor while crew ashore - towed into Penzance by ILB.

8/08/03 : **ILB** Swimmer believed to be in difficulties - found to be OK.

11/08/03 : **ILB** Windsurfer in difficulties behind Newlyn quay - found to be OK

12/08/03 : **ILB** Search for missing boy off Marazion - found to be OK.

14/08/03 : **ILB** Call to assist yacht *Quest* off Penzance - both crew elderly and injured - towed in to Penzance.

16/08/03 : **ILB** Yacht stranded in Mousehole harbour mouth - ILB attended, and again at high tide to assist yacht off.

19/08/03 : **ILB** Canoe reported on St Clement's Island with no owner - owner found to be there and OK.

22/08/03 : **ILB & ALB** Sailing dinghy reported overdue from Mousehole - dinghy found off St Michael's Mount - escorted to Mousehole by ILB.

25/08/03 : **ILB** Small cabin cruiser *BJ* seen dragging anchor off Penzance harbour - towed in to Penzance.

3/09/03 : **ILB** Swimmer seen making distress signal from St Clement's Island - reported unable to swim back due to harassment by seal - taken back to Mousehole.

13/09/03 : **ILB** Children reported cut off on Chapel Rock, Marazion - escorted to shore.

(Roy Pascoe collection).

PENZANCE

Lifeboat *Alexandra*

1865	Jan 29	Brig *Willie Ridley* of Plymouth,	saved	8

Lifeboat *Richard Lewis*

1865	Nov 24	Brigantine *Tobaco* of Hamburg,	saved	5
1866	Jan 11	SS *Bessie* of Hayle,	saved	5
1867	Jan 5	Schooner *Salome* of Dartmouth,	saved	6
		Brigantine *Selina Ann* of Fowey	saved	5
		Schooner *Heiress* of Teignmouth,	saved	6
	Jan 7	Ship *John Gray* of Glasgow,	saved	13
	Mar 17	Brig *Secret* of Guernsey,	placed pilot on board	
1868	Dec 6	Barque *North Britain* of Southampton,	saved	8
1873	Jan 26	Brig *Otto* of Moss,	saved	8
	Feb 2	Schooner *Marie Emilie* of Lorient,	saved	4
1879	May 17	Brig *Ponthieu* of Vannes,	saved	5
1881	Feb 14	Ship *Macduff* of Glasgow,	assisted to save vessel	
	Sep 5	Barquentine *Neilly* of Bridgwater,	assisted to save vessel and	6
	Nov 24/25	Barque *Pampero* of Swansea,	assisted to save vessel and	14

Lifeboat *Dora*

1885	Jan 31	Barque *Petrellen* of Porsgrund,	saved	8
	Feb 1	Barque *Petrellen* of Porsgrund,	saved	10
	Apr 24/25	Fishing boats of Penzance,	stood by	
1886	Dec 8	Dandy *Alliance* of Penzance,	saved	4
		Schooner *Golden Light* of Penzance,	saved	5
1888	May 17	Brigantine *Jeune Hortense* of Nantes,	saved	4
	Nov 8	Schooner *Livingstone* of Lancaster,	saved	5
1889	Jan 29	Trawler *Blue Bell* of Plymouth,	saved	4
1890	Dec 31	Brig *Dorothy* of North Shields,	assisted to save vessel and	8
1891	Mar 10	Schooner *Joseph Nicholson* of Newcastle,	saved vessel and	5
1892	Oct 15	Schooner *Express* of Dublin	saved vessel and	4

Lifeboat *Elizabeth and Blanche I*

1896	Dec 8	Saved a man blown from the sea wall		
1897	Mar 4	Barque *Lady Gladys* of Tonsberg,	saved	17
1898	Feb 25	Schooner *Mary James* of Penzance,	saved	10
	Mar 25	Brigantine *Henry Harvey* of Hayle,	saved	6

Lifeboat *Elizabeth and Blanche II*

1901	Mar 29	Barque *Antarctic* of Swansea,	landed	9
	Dec 23	Brigantine *St Joseph* of Lannion,	assisted to save vessel	
1907	Sep 27	SS *Ellesmere* of Manchester,	took doctor to steamer	

Lifeboat *Cape of Good Hope*

1909	Feb 21	Steam drifter *Renown* of Yarmouth,	saved vessel and	9

Lifeboat *Janet Hoyle*

1912	Dec 26	SS *Tripolitania* of Genoa,	no service	
1913	Mar 21	Steam & sailing trawlers entering harbour,	stood by	

NEWLYN

Lifeboat *Elizabeth and Blanche II*

1908	Dec 28	Ship *Clan MacPherson* of Glasgow,	saved	20
		Schooner *Titania* of Salcombe,	rendered assistance	
1910	Feb 19	Ketch trawler *Radiance* of Brixham,	stood by	
	Oct 14	Schooner *Lizzie* of Weymouth,	stood by	
1911	Jan 12/13	Schooner *Lizzie Ellen* of Cardigan,	helped vessel to safety	
	Apr 29	SS *Cragoswald* of Newcastle,	saved	27
	Oct 13	SS *Hammershus* of Copenhagen,	assisted to save vessel	
	Dec 13	Barque *Saluto* of Christiansand,	saved	13
	Dec 21	SS *Hellopes* of Liverpool,	saved	4
1912	Feb 11	Barque *Etoile Polaire* of Fecamp,	saved vessel and	8
	Feb 28/29	SS *Northlands* of Cardiff,	stood by & assisted to save vessel	
Mar 13		SS *South America* of London,	stood by	

PENLEE

Lifeboat *Elizabeth and Blanche II*

1914	Oct 22	SS *Liguria* of Genoa,	assisted to save vessel	
1915	Oct 27/28	Ketch *Traly* of Tralee,	assisted to save vessel and	6
1917	Apr 11	SS *West Wales* of Cardiff,	assisted to save vessel	
1918	Nov 4	H.M.Tug *Epic*,	stood by	
	Nov 5	H.M.Tug *Epic*,	saved	17
1922	Jan 24	SS *Gracefield* of Swansea,	stood by	
	Jul 8	SS *Concordia* of Genoa,	stood by	

Lifeboat *The Brothers*

1923	Jan 3	SS *Dubravka* of Dubrovnik,	saved	27
	Sep 30	SS *Nicolas Norbett* of Boulogne,	stood by and piloted to Newlyn	
	Oct 8	SS *City of Westminster* of Liverpool,	saved	35
1924	Aug 5	SS *River Ely* of Cardiff,	rendered assistance and landed	5
1925	Sep 29	Steam trawler *Rig* of Ramsgate,	saved vessel	
1928	Oct 27	SS *Mona* of Antwerp,	escorted vessel to safety	

Lifeboat *W & S*

1931	Sep 5	SS *Opal* of Glasgow,	recovered a body	
1935	Nov 30	Motor fishing boat *Adventure* of Penzance,	saved boat and	5
	Dec 8	SS *Cornish Rose* of Liverpool,	assisted to save vessel and	9
1936	Jan 27	SS *Taycraig* of London,	saved	9
	Jun 19	Motor fishing boat *Gleaner* of Penzance,	escorted boat to safety	
1937	Jan 11	Motor trawler *Vierge Marie* of Ostend,	recovered 2 bodies and saved	1
	Oct 20	Motor fishing boat *Apapa* of Newlyn,	saved boat and	1
1938	Apr 22	Steam fishing boat *Pioneer* of Penzance,	towed in boat and saved	2
1939	Jan 31	Motor trawler *Paul Therese* of Ostend,	saved vessel and	6
1940	Feb 7	Motor trawler *Jeannine* of Ostend,	escorted vessel to safety	
	Feb 21	SS *Westown* of London,	escorted to harbour	

Reserve Lifeboat *B. A. S. P.*

1940	Mar 17	SS *Miervaldis* of Riga,	gave help	

Lifeboat *W & S*

1941	Feb 2/3	SS *Heire* of Oslo,	stood by	
	Mar 8	SS *Margo* of Cardiff,	1st service landed 3 and 1 body, 2nd service landed 2, 3rd service rendered assistance	
	Mar 8	SS *Falkvik* of Solvesborg,	landed 1 wounded man	
1942	Apr 24	Fishing boats *Margaret, Boy Dan* and *Alsace Lorraine* of Newlyn,	saved three boats and	12
1943	Aug 20	Dutch motor vessel,	stood by	
1944	Jan 6	SS *Solstad* of Norrkoping,	saved	14
1945	Jan 3	SS *Strait Fisher* of Cardiff,	saved empty boat	
	Mar 21	SS *John R Park* of San Francisco,	stood by	
	Mar 26	MV *Pacific* of Groningen,	saved ship's boat	
	Mar 29	H.M.C.S. *Teme* (K 458),	landed	57
	Dec 18	Yacht *Diane* of Cowes,	saved yacht and	7
1947	Apr 23	Obsolete warship *Warspite*,	saved	8
1948	Feb 7	Wolf Rock Lighthouse,	stood by while supplies were dropped	
	Jun 7		landed bodies of 2 bathers	
1949	Sep 4	Customs motor launch *Badger*,	stood by while towed to harbour	
	Sep 19	Sea Otter Seaplane,	stood by	

Reserve Lifeboat *M. O. Y E.*

1950	Jul 15	Salvage vessel *Barnet*,	landed 5 from tug *Freebooter*	
	Nov 11	Tug *Masterman* of Falmouth,	stood by	

Lifeboat *W & S*

1951	Jan 27	Post Office cable ship *Ariel*,	landed a sick man and 2 doctors	
1952	Oct 25	Seven Stones Light Vessel,	landed a keeper	
1955	Oct 13	SS *Manolito* of Puerto Limon,	landed an injured man	
1956	Mar 1	MV *Crete Avon* of London,	stood by and gave help	
	Mar 14	Trawler *Vert Prairial* of Dieppe,	recovered 2 bodies	

Reserve Lifeboat *Millie Walton*

1956	Jul 8	SS *Yewcroft* of Glasgow,	saved	10

Lifeboat *W & S*

1956	Nov 6	SS *Pontoporus* of Piraeus,	took out a doctor, saving	1
	Dec 9	MV *Harborough* of London,	landed an injured man	
1957	Mar 10		recoverd a rubber dinghy	
	Jul 29	S. tanker *Cnosa* of Monrovia,	landed an injured man	
	Sep 18	SS *Alexandria*,	landed an injured man	
	Dec 25	M. tanker *Hemisinus* of London,	landed an injured man	
1958	Aug 15	Motor fishing vessel *Hesperian* of Penzance,	saved vessel and	6
1959	Feb 2	SS *Asia* of Liverpool,	landed a sick man	
	Apr 1	Crabber *Pluie de Roses* of Audierne,	landed	4
	Jul 19	SS *Lindi* of Antwerp,	landed a sick man	
	Sep 12	MV *San Blas* of Stockholm,	landed an injured man	
	Sep 23	Tanker *London Resolution* of London,	landed an injured man	
1960	Feb 18	Fishing boat *May* (SS347) of St Ives,	saved boat and	1
	May 8	Seven Stones Light Vessel,	landed a sick man	
	May 19	MV *Saarland* of Vagesack,	landed a sick man from H.M.S. *Undine*	
	May 25	MV *Sangara* of Liverpool,	landed sick woman and baby	
	Jun 15	MV *Rowallan Castle* of London,	landed a sick man	

Lifeboat *Solomon Browne*

	Sep 25	MV *Fravizo* of Amsterdam,	landed a woman and a baby	
	Sep 27	Tanker *Belmare* of Gothenburg,	landed a body	
1961	Jan 4	MV *Mille Heering* of Copenhagen,	landed a sick man	
	Feb 18	MV *Leersum* of Amsterdam,	landed a sick man	
	May 17	SS *Olympos* of Piraeus,	landed a sick man	
	May 25	Yacht *Susan* of Penzance,	saved boat and	2
	Jun 16	MV *Doreifs* of Monrovia,	landed a sick child	
	Jun 25	MV *La Colina* of London,	landed an injured man	
	Jun 25	SS *Mergus* of Helsingborg,	landed a sick man	
	Aug 15	Tanker *Kent* of London,	landed a sick man	
	Sep 15	MV *King Charles* of London,	landed a sick man	
	Sep 24	MV *Iron Horse* of Newcastle,	landed a sick man	
	Dec 12	Tanker *Border Falcon* of Newcastle,	landed a sick man	
	Dec 18	MV *Naess Pioneer* of London,	embarked 2 and landed 2, saving	1
	Dec 27	SS *Okeanis* of Piraeus,	landed a sick man	
	Dec 30	Tanker *Varicella* of London,	landed a sick man	
1962	Mar 5	SS *River Afton* of Newcastle,	landed an injured man	
	May 5	Tanker *Haminella* of London,	landed 2 sick men	
	Sep 1	MV *Ben Hope* of Leith,	landed 2 injured men	
	Sep 9	MV *Uskport* of Newport,	landed a sick man	
	Dec 3	Tug *Ocean Bull* of Ostend,	landed a sick man	
1963	Feb 27	MV *Livanita* of Grimstad,	landed a sick man	
	Apr 13	Motor boat *Ranger*,	gave help	
	Aug 21	Troopship *Upshur* of San Francisco,	landed a sick man	
	Oct 12	SS *American Merchant* of New York,	landed a sick man	
	Oct 23	MV *Juan Ferrer* of Valencia,	landed a body and saved	1
1964	May 7	Fishing boat *Sheila* of Newlyn,	in difficulties off Praa Sands, escorted to Newlyn	
	May 12	Tanker *Haminea* of London,	landed injured master	
	Nov 19	MV *Clarkeden* of London,	landed an injured man	
1965	Jan 1	United States MV *American Skipper*,	landed a sick man	
	Jan 4	West German MV *Clipper*,	landed a sick man	
	Apr 17	Rubber dinghy and small launch,	saved two boats and	4
	Jun 12	Greek MV *Eurylochus* of Piraeus,	landed a sick man	
	Aug 28	MV *Cavallo* of Hull,	landed a sick stewardess	
	Aug 29	Tanker *Verconella* of London,	landed an injured man	
	Sep 28	Tanker *London Harmony*,	landed an injured man	
	Nov 11	Belgian trawler *Erna*,	recovered wreckage	
	Nov 26	Trawlers *Jacqueline* and *Trewarveneth* of Newlyn,	escorted boats in tow of two trawlers	
1966	Jan 4	French trawler *Yves Chantal*,	gave help	
	Mar 9	MV *Silver Comet*,	landed an injured man	
	Mar 11	MV *Clan McIver*,	landed a sick man	
	Mar 21	Danish MV *Dangule Maersk* of Copenhagen,	landed 2 injured men	
	Mar 29	Greek MV *Proodos*,	landed a sick man	
	Apr 10	Liberian tanker *G.S.Livanos*,	landed a sick woman	
	May 29	Dutch MV *Oranje Nassau*,	landed an injured man	
	Jul 6	Tanker *Alnair* of Monrovia,	landed a sick man	
	Aug 24	MV *Baltana* of Norway,	landed a sick man	
	Sep 10	MV *Ramadhan*,	landed a sick man	
	Sep 29	Sick man on board MV *Dunedin Star*,	landed a sick man	
	Oct 1	MV *Ems Ore* of Monrovia,	took police and doctor to ship and returned with doctor	
	Nov 19	MV *Beaver Ash* of London,	landed a sick man	
	Dec 25	Tanker *Saga Surf* of Oslo,	landed a sick man	
	Dec 31	Ore carrier *Monksgarth* of London,	took out doctor	

1967	Jan 22	MV *Kohima*, landed a sick man		
	Mar 19	Tanker *Torrey Canyon* of Monrovia,	stood by vessel	
	May 6	MV *Clivia* of Bremen,	landed a sick man	
	Jun 23	MV *King Alexander* of London,	landed an injured man	
	Jul 22	Sailing dinghy,	rescued	1
	Aug 1	Tanker *Tahchee* of Panama,	landed 2 injured men	
	Sep 12	Fishing boat *Onward*,	gave help	
	Sep 22	MV *Paul Endacott* of Trellberg,	landed a sick man	
	Dec 6	Tanker *Al-Sabbiyah* of Kuwait,	landed a sick child	
	Dec 19	Ore carrier *Trinculo* of London,	landed a sick man	
1968	Feb 24	Tanker M*arietta* of Monrovia,	landed an injured man	
	Apr 12	MV *Eumaeus* of Amsterdam,	landed an injured man	
	May 28	Sick man on board SS *Cotopaxi* of Liverpool,	took out doctor	
	Jun 29	Dutch liner *Ryndam* of Waterman,	landed a sick girl	
	Jul 11	Fishing boat *My Girl*,	gave help	
	Dec 10	Tanker *Eridge* of London,	landed a sick man	
1969	Jan 17	MV *Firth Fisher* of Barrow,	stood by vessel	

Reserve Lifeboat *Thomas McCunn*

	Apr 15	Ore carrier *Trinculo* of London,	landed a sick man	
	May 17	Yacht *Silver Thistle*,	saved boat and	3
	Aug 1	Sick man on board French trawler *Jean Marie*,	took out doctor	
	Aug 19	Tanker *Georgian Glory* of Piraeus,	landed a sick man	

Lifeboat *Solomon Browne*

1970	Feb 22	Tug *Friesland*,	landed an injured man	
	Apr 30	MV *Cape Rodney* of Glasgow,	landed a sick man	
	May 29	MY *Malta Faith*,	landed a sick man	
	Aug 11	MY *Methane Progress* of London,	landed a sick man	
	Dec 2	MFV *Anthony Stevenson*,	saved vessel and	5
1971	Jan 15	R.N. helicopter,	recovered wreckage	
	Feb 2	Tanker *Prima*,	landed a sick man	
	Mar 29	Ore carrier *La Chacra* of London,	took out a doctor and landed a sick man	
	Apr 11	MV *Freiburg* of Hamburg,	took out a doctor	
	May 27	Fishing boat *Cornish Supreme*,	gave help	
	Jul 21	Motor launch *Silver Dolphin*,	saved boat and	2
	Aug 1	Motor launch,	gave help	
	Aug 10	Motor launch *Doona*,	saved boat and	2
	Aug 10	Tanker *Mistral* of Helsinki,	landed a sick man	
	Sep 7	Fishing boat *Alma*,	gave help	
	Sep 29	MV *Valle de Butron*,	landed a sick man, thereby saving a life	
1972	Feb 14	Sick man on board MV *Finnmaid* of Helsinki,	landed a sick man	
	Mar 26	Fishing boat *Golden Corn* of St Ives,	gave help	
	Apr 6	Fishing boat *Lead On* of Penzance,	saved boat and	2
	Apr 16	MFV *Mary Ellen* of Penzance,	gave help	
	May 8	Sick man on board tanker *Mandan* of Hamburg,	landed a sick man	
	Jun 22	Fishing boat *Talisman* of Penzance,	escorted boat	
	Aug 1	Man fallen over cliff,	rescued	
	Oct 16	MFV *Sadie Wykeham*,	saved boat and	2
	Oct 16	Fishing boat *Golden Corn*,	saved boat and	2
	Oct 17	Sick man on board MV *C.P.Trader* of London,	landed a sick man	
	Nov 5	Sick man on board MV *Seconda* of London,	took out doctor and landed sick man	
	Dec 17	MFV *Girl Sybil* of Penzance,	saved boat and	4
1973	Jun 13	Fishing boat *Louise PZ 271*,	saved boat and	2

	Jul 10	Motor boat *Apolo* of Penzance,	saved boat and	9
	Jul 17	Injured man on board trawler		
		Big Cat of Brixham,	took out doctor	
	Sep 1	FV *Morwylas* of Penzance,	saved boat and	3
	Sep 8	Trawler *Joan Swallow*,	gave help	
	Sep 18	Fishing vessel *Fiona Mary*,	escorted boat	
	Dec 15	FV *Kingfisher* of Falmouth,	gave help	
1974	Apr 13	Power boat *Zodiac*,	gave help	
	Jun 9	MFV *Barlow* of St Ives,	gave help	
	Jul 12	Auxiliary yacht *Le Stringo* of London,	escorted boat	
	Dec 15	MFV *Nimrod*,	gave help	
1975	Jan 25	MV *Lovat*,	landed 5 bodies	

Reserve Lifeboat *Gertrude*

	Jun 8	MFV *Margaret Ann*,	saved boat and	2

Lifeboat *Solomon Browne*

	Dec 2	Trawler *Enfant de Bretagne*,	escorted vessels in tow of trawler	
	Dec 9	FV *Green Cormorant* of Penzance,	gave help	
1976	Jul 30	FV *Linella* of Newlyn,	gave help	
	Aug 1	FV *Streak* of Penzance,	gave help	
	Oct 21	FV *Monarch*,	gave help	
	Nov 16	Sick person on board trawler		
		Kristyan Rand of Russia,	took out doctor	
1977	Jun 13	Helicopter,	recovered wreckage	
	Aug 13	Yacht *Esperancia* of Brazil,	stood by boat	
	Aug 14	Sick person on board motor launch *Windelf*,	landed a sick person	
	Sep 10	Trawler *Kerlano* of France,	rescued	1
	Sep 16	Yacht *Flamina* of Harlech,	saved boat and	4
	Dec 27	Trawler *Conqueror* of Grimsby,	rescued	15
	Dec 28	do,	stood by vessel	
		do,	rescued	3
		do,	rescued	3
1978	May 4	Yacht *Slipalong*,	saved boat and	2
	May 11	FV *Janette Elaine* of St Ives,	escorted vessel	
	Jun 23	FV *Emu*,	saved vessel and	3
	Dec 17	FV *Karenza Mor* of Falmouth,	escorted vessel	
1979	Jan 18	Sick man on board carrier	took out doctor	
		Nordic Louisiana of London,	and landed a sick man	
	Feb 13	Catamaran *Juro Doje*,	gave help	
	Apr 29	FV *Sleep Robber* of Falmouth,	saved vessel and	2
	May 10	FV *Conquest* of Plymouth,	escorted vessel	
	Jun 2	Yacht *Margaret Jane*,	escorted boat	
	Aug 2	MFV *Hazel* of London,	saved boat and	3
	Aug 16	Yacht *Gan*,	gave help	
	Aug 27	Trawler *Paliria* of France,	landed	6
	Sep 1	Two injured men on board container	took out doctor and	
		vessel *Sealand Market* of U.S.A.,	landed 1 injured man	
	Sep 4	FV *Box Michael* of Penzance, gave help		
	Oct 5	Yacht *Run Wild*,	gave help	
1980	Mar 19	MFV *Normauwil* of Belgium,	saved vessel and	7
	Mar 31	Yacht *Pascaul Flores* of Bristol,	escorted vessel	
	Apr 15	Yacht *Forge Rival* of Milford,	gave help	

Reserve Lifeboat *Jesse Lumb*

	Oct 16	Injured man on board trawler *Roche Blanche* of France,	took out doctor and escorted vessel	
	Nov 26	Injured man on board MFV *Silver Harvester* of Penzance,	took out doctor and escorted vessel	
1981	Apr 13	FV *Frim* of Penzance,	saved vessel and	4
	Jun 28	Catamaran,	gave help	
	Aug 6	FV *Emma* of Penzance,	gave help	
	Sep 6	FV *Jumbo* of Penzance,	gave help	
	Dec 8	FV *Quo Vadis*,	gave help	
	Dec 19	Cargo vessel *Union Star*	gave help	

The lifeboat having taken off four people was wrecked attempting to save the remaining four people with the loss of her entire crew who were awarded RNLI medals for gallantry as follows:

Coxswain William Trevelyan Richards	Gold Medal
Second Coxswain/ Mechanic James Stephen Madron	Bronze Medal
Assistant Mechanic Nigel Brockman	Bronze Medal
Emergency Mechanic John Robert Blewett	Bronze Medal
Crew Member Charles Thomas Greenhaugh	Bronze Medal
Crew Member Kevin Smith	Bronze Medal
Crew Member Barrie Robertson Torrie	Bronze Medal
Crew Member Gary Lee Wallis	Bronze Medal

COXSWAINS

C	1860 – 1873	Thomas Carbis
C	1873 – 1896	Henry Trewhella
	1896 – 1904	Phillip Nichols
	1903 – 1906	George Chirgwin
	1907 – 1908	Alfred Vingoe
	1908 – 1912 (Penzance)	Charles Tredwin
	1908 – 1910 (Newlyn)	Alfred Vingoe
	1910 – 1913 (Newlyn)	T.E. Vingoe
	1912 – 1915 (Penzance)	W. Nicholls
	1913 – 1916 (Penlee)	J.S. Brownfield
	1915 (Penzance)	Joe Hill
	1915 – 1917 (Penzance)	Robert Harvey
	1916 – 1920 (Penlee -)	G. Dennis
	1920 – 1947	Frank Blewett
	1947 – 1957	Edwin F. Madron
	1957 – 1970	John T. (Jack) Worth
	1970 – 1981	W. Trevelyan Richards
	1982 – 1992	Ken Thomas
	1992	Neil Brockman

HONORARY SECRETARIES

1826 – 1862	Richard Pearce
1863 – 1864	Cmndr. C. J. Austin RN
1864 – 1866	W. D. Matthews Jr.
1866 – 1875	Nicholas B. Downing
1875 – 1882	John Matthews
1882 – 1886	Frederick C. Matthews
1886 – 1913	Col. T. H. Cornish
1913 – 1917	Barrie B. Bennetts
1917 – 1919	Capt. J. Sincock
1919 – 1957	Barrie B. Bennetts
1957 – 1964	J. K. Bennetts
1964 – 1989	D. L. Johnson
1989 –	Andrew Munson

BRANCH VOLUNTEER AWARDS

Mrs C. F. Bazeley	1977	Statuette
Mr J. K. Bennetts	1964	Binoculars
Mr B. B. Bennetts	1948	Gold Badge
Mr B. B. Bennetts	1957	Honorary Life Governor
Mr C. G. B. Bennetts	1984	Silver Badge
Mrs I. M. Blake	1970	Silver Badge
Mrs E. Bushby	2003	Certificate of Thanks
Mr J. Corin	1988	Statuette
Mr P. Garnier	1998	Statuette
Capt. R. E. Goodman	1972	Silver Badge
Mrs A. M. Goodman	1990	Statuette
Dr M. Hersant	1994	Silver Badge
Dr M. Hersant	2005	Gold Badge
Dr P. Hicks	2003	Statuette
Mr J. Hodge	1980	Silver badge
Mr J. Hodge	1990	Gold badge
Miss C. James	1977	Silver Badge
Mr D. L. Johnson	1987	Gold Badge
Mr D. L. Johnson	1996	Bar to Gold Badge
Mr D. L. Johnson	2002	Honorary Life Governor
Mrs R. Johnson	1998	Gold badge
Mrs R. Johnson	2003	Bar to Gold Badge
Mr A. O. Kernick	1949	Statuette
Mr A. O. Kernick	1952	Binoculars
Mr A. O. Kernick	1972	Bar to Gold Badge
Dr D. W. L. Leslie	1972	Silver Badge
Dr D. W. L. Leslie	1982	Gold Badge
Mrs J. Madron	2000	Silver Badge
Mr R. Morris	1988	Certificate of Thanks
Mr A. Munson	2000	Binoculars
Mrs E. Roberts	1994	Certificate of Thanks
Mrs E. L. Smith	1980	Statuette
Miss R. Wallen	1987	Silver Badge
Mrs B. Wallen	2003	Gold Badge
Mrs M. Wallen	1990	Silver Badge
Mrs M. Williams	1977	Silver Badge